D1134931

EVANGELICAL RESPONSIBILITY IN CONTEMPORARY THEOLOGY

PATHWAY BOOKS

A SERIES OF CONTEMPORARY EVANGELICAL STUDIES

All Ye That Labor
by Lester DeKoster

The Pattern of Authority
by Bernard Ramm

When the Time Had Fully Come
by Herman N. Ridderbos

Is There a Conflict Between Genesis 1 *and Natural Science?*
by Nicolaas H. Ridderbos

Man in Nature and in Grace
by Stuart Barton Babbage

Archaeology and the Old Testament
by J. A. Thompson

Out of the Earth (*Archaeology and the N. T.*)
by E. M. Blaiklock

Preaching and Biblical Theology
by Edmund P. Clowney

Sacramental Teaching and Practice in the Reformation Churches
by G. W. Bromiley

Who Wrote Isaiah?
by Edward J. Young

BIOGRAPHICAL NOTE

CARL F. H. HENRY, Professor of Systematic Theology and Christian Philosophy at Fuller Theological Seminary, has taken leave of absence from his seminary post to become Editor of *Christianity Today*. Over a period of many years Dr. Henry has been a student and teacher of both philosophy and theology. He has also been a writer. Among his books are: *Remaking the Modern Mind, The Uneasy Conscience of Modern Fundamentalism, The Protestant Dilemma.* His major work in the field of philosophy and theology has recently been published under the title, *Christian Personal Ethics.*

Evangelical Responsibility in Contemporary Theology

BY

CARL F. H. HENRY
Professor of Systematic Theology and Christian Philosophy
Fuller Theological Seminary

WM. B. EERDMANS PUBLISHING COMPANY
GRAND RAPIDS, MICHIGAN

Library of Congress catalog card number: 57-13036
Printed in the United States of America
First printing, September 1957

GENERAL INTRODUCTION

PATHWAY BOOKS are designed to help teachers, students, preachers, and laymen keep themselves informed on the important subjects and the crucial problems which confront the Christian church today. They are designed to help the reader bear witness to the Christian faith in the modern world.

Consulting Editors for Pathway Books are: F. F. Bruce, Head of the Department of Biblical History and Literature, University of Sheffield, England, and Editor of *The Evangelical Quarterly;* Leon Morris, Vice-Principal of Ridley College, Melbourne, Australia; Bernard Ramm, Director of Graduate Studies in Religion, Baylor University, Waco, Texas; and Edward J. Young, Professor of Old Testament, Westminster Theological Seminary, Philadelphia, Pennsylvania.

The writer of each volume is, of course, solely responsible for the opinions and judgments expressed in his book. The Consulting Editors give valuable suggestions and advice, but the choice of subject and author, and the general direction of the series is the responsibility of the publisher.

CONTENTS

PREFACE

TODAY THE FORCES of irreligion hold the initiative in three-fifths of the world. Against this tide, democratic powers increasingly emphasize the religious basis of freedom. To assail the Communist disparagement of religion as an opiate of the masses, the free world assumes more and more the brotherhood or essential kinship of all religions. In this placid climate of events, denominational debate, Protestant polemics, and competitive missions threaten to build the thunderheads of religious feuding. Within Protestantism itself, in our generation, the great barometer of church history is registering toward conciliation and union. The ecumenical forecast of pan-Protestant cooperation has sounded over our fast-moving century, to diminish the pressure of divisiveness that has vexed Protestantism since the Reformation.

Outlining this dream of a giant church we note both spiritually unifying and tactically competitive factors. To fulfill the Lord's high-priestly prayer "that they may all be one" has become a major incentive to Protestant unity. An added pressure is the specter of growing Roman Catholic political power in America, which dramatizes the advantages of a central voice speaking for the scattered and isolated churches. Some denominations have seen the possibility of merging with related denominations at no cost to doctrinal essentials. Others have found new stimulus in supra-denominational fellowships of one form or another. Intolerant of religious debate and fragmentation, the temper of the times is overtly predisposed to cooperation and concord. Should we not hope that in the realm of religion we may find a way to resolve differences in a spirit of love? Since it is precisely the Hebrew-Christian religion that uncompromisingly enjoins its followers to neighbor-love, should we not be properly indignant over some warring chapters in the total history of Christianity? Are there not accusing paragraphs in the segment of Protestant history, and especially in recent contemporary history? Would we not all wish to delete them from the indelible annals of our times? Such is the ecclesiastical mood and movement that supplies the setting of our century for evaluating evangelical responsibility in contemporary theology.

The ultimate fate of Protestantism, shadowed throughout the West by two generations of theological turmoil, remains in doubt. In America this clash of Protestant perspectives took the form of the modernist-fundamentalist controversy, a fixing of positions from which theological debate is now only gradually disengaging itself. Whether present realignments are gain or loss, whether disputed positions of the past are best formulated in some new way – these are but variant phrasings of a current theological concern: Shall we revive the modernist-fundamentalist controversy?

The most important fact to be fixed in sketching responsibility in theology is that of Christian fidelity. Necessarily and unavoidably, this involves the delicate task of spiritual judgment. Academic lectures, unfortunately, do not always provide comprehensive solutions to burdensome ecclesiastical problems. But perhaps the minimal service expected of them is that they contribute somewhat to the clarification of perspectives. This fond hope motivates these lectures on *Evangelical Responsibility in Contemporary Theology*. In trust that Christian loyalties may be thereby strengthened, I shall consider the fortunes of Protestantism in our era under the successive themes of The Modernist Revision, The Fundamentalist Reduction, The Contemporary Restoration, and The Evangelical Responsibility.

I wish to express my appreciation to the faculty of Northern Baptist Theological Seminary in Chicago for the opportunity of presenting these lectures as the 1957 Wilkinson Lecture series (April 30-May 3, 1957), and to the leadership of the Christian Reformed Church for the opportunity of presenting them as Centennial Lectures (June 4-7, 1957) during the centennial anniversary year of that Church. My appreciation is also due my secretary, Miss Irma Peterson, for the preparation of the index.

CARL F. H. HENRY

Washington, D.C.

EVANGELICAL RESPONSIBILITY IN CONTEMPORARY THEOLOGY

CHAPTER ONE

THE MODERNIST REVISION

WHOEVER EVALUATES the modernist-fundamentalist controversy from the standpoint of the sixth decade of the twentieth century must sense the current distaste for religious contention, must sense the deference to ecumenical cooperation. In the face of present pressures for unity and unanimity, the ministry no doubt reflects an increasing impatience with controversy because of its apparent historical futility. Ecumenical inclusivism rolls on; each passing year registers new mergers and numerical gains while the minority outside diminishes. Since many churchmen dismiss "contending for the faith" as an unnecessary contentiousness in today's world, what value lies in adding controversy to this wave of misunderstanding? Is it not possible in a spirit of love to maintain a merely formal identification with ecumenical forces, or at least an attitude of quiescent indifference, while at the same time preserving an isolated self-contained community witness? For is it not at this local level, after all, that every city and hamlet must ultimately work out its own salvation?

An added pressure is the destructive impact of religious controversy upon the unchurched multitudes. For more than half a century liberal preaching defined the evangelical message as irrelevant and meaningless for modern man. Conservative pulpits, in turn, affirmed that whatever else modernism might be, it was not Christianity. As the decades passed, increasing multitudes detached themselves from the churches. All the while modernist inveighed against fundamentalist and fundamentalist against modernist. Within the twentieth century two generations of conflict rocked Protestant pulpits and pews with theological debate oriented primarily to those inside the churches. Accordingly, the unchurched multitudes have been watching from the sidelines, justifying their detachment from a pugilistic spirituality. To those who find no peace in the world outside, cannot Protestant Christianity in this century's third generation offer at least the prospect of a spiritual fellowship of peace?

Alongside these pressures against church strife engendered out of consideration for the larger Protestant witness and for the unchurched masses, evangelicals within their own camp experienced unexpected disappointments because of religious controversy. While deploring the calculating strategy that delivered one influential post after another to liberal denominational leadership, conservatives saw some of their own leaders fall prey to the lust for ecclesiastical prominence and power. Theological controversy got out of hand; not only was it appended to personal ambition, but it was made to serve unnecessary discord and division. Once united on doctrinal essentials against those who denied these essentials, evangelical believers and churches now were thrown into debate over non-essentials. The positive side of theological controversy (the case for great Christian beliefs) was yielded swiftly to the negative. Pulpit and convention became a platform for the denunciation of personalities and organizations. Fundamentalist strategy became shorn of perspective, tolerance, and charity. Thus deployed to a negative and reactionary approach, the evangelical movement forfeited much of its great opportunity to proclaim the distinctively Christian doctrines compellingly. In the course of preserving their Christian heritage, the fundamentalist churches were lured from their task of positive preaching.

Another reason to resist a renewal of modernist-fundamentalist debate centers in the present upsurge in church attendance by the spiritually illiterate. Bewildered by an inner uncertainty, insecurity, and fear in the aftermath of two global wars, the American people now throng the churches in record numbers. Most of these churchgoers are unfamiliar with the history of the modernist-fundamentalist controversy. Before they are invited to saving faith in Christ, shall they learn unhappy details of the past generation's theological and ecclesiastical tension and trouble? Does not the present theological state warrant indicting a fundamentalist who uses his pulpit merely to flay the old liberalism? Likewise, does not the liberal minister reveal a telling ignorance of present issues when he speaks of evangelical Christianity only in terms of the objectionable features of the old fundamentalism? To keep the fire of faith burning brightly for those who throng the tabernacles of God today, dare we neglect a new perspective on the recent past?

Thus far we have dealt mainly with a mid-century ministerial mood and mind-set, namely, an aversion to perpetuating the modernist-fundamentalist debate. Because of the modern premium on ecclesiastical unity, because of the inelegant impression church controversy makes upon the world, because of the easy degeneration of theological conflict into negation and lovelessness, and because of the rising generation of churchgoers who must be linked swiftly with the first generation of Christian faith, there is a growing impatience today with the effort to preserve the edge of the past generation's theological debate as the permanent center of Christian polemics, apologetics, and evangelism.

This impatience is by no means universal, however. In some circles the ecclesiastical encounter still follows the same lines shaped a generation or two ago. Usually the hinterlands learn only slowly of changing emphases in the contemporary outlook. In the remote rural areas and in the smaller cities, modernist and fundamentalist ministers often remain quite out of touch with influential re-evaluations of their traditions; the situation of a previous generation continues to formulate their convictions. This disposition to gauge contemporary Protestantism in terms of the bygone modernist-fundamentalist debate is not limited to rural religion, however; it is shared also by some influential leaders who are otherwise quite abreast of the current religious drift. Some vocal fundamentalists consider the modernist-fundamentalist divide the permanent razor edge to which all the destinies of twentieth-century Christianity must be exposed. This view is encouraged by men of not insignificant influence in opinion-forming media – church councils, periodicals, schools, exclusivist movements. Whatever loss of influence in evangelical circles may overtake such men, at mid-century they symbolize fundamentalism in a dual sense – as a theological perspective and as a subjective temperament, which regards as its enemy anything outside its own bounds.

The fundamentalist wing is not alone, however, in the tendency to perpetuate the fundamentalist-modernist controversy. Even some liberals draw the lines of ecclesiastical dispute much as was done a generation ago. They refuse to share Karl Barth's and Emil Brunner's sharp criticism of classic liberal theology. No less a modernist than Harry Emerson Fosdick believes that the fate of Christianity still reduces to a necessary conflict between the old liberalism and fundamentalism. In 1922 Dr. Fosdick's sermon "Shall the Fundamentalists Win?" made him the storm center of American preaching. Three decades later his highly readable autobiography *The Living of These Days* (New York: Harper, 1957) spins a halo of self-justification over Dr. Fosdick's vagabondage and endeavors to vindicate the liberalism to which he raised an altar.* Dr. Fosdick guards his cherished liberalism from any need for repentance and radical revision. Likewise his verdict on fundamentalism is identical to that of thirty years ago. He dismissed it then as reactionary Christianity "tempted to retreat into hidebound obscurantism, denying the discoveries of science, and insisting on the literal acceptance of every biblical idea" (p. 144); as "one of the worst exhibitions of bitter intolerance" (p. 145), "fighting mad" (p. 147), "the flare-up of a rear-guard action" (p. 164), "out-dated thinking" (p. 165). The evangelicals he quotes are almost always of an immoderate and uncharitable variety, given at times even to personal abuse. In a name-studded volume of more than 300 pages, Dr. Fosdick nowhere mentions J. Gresham Machen, doubtless the outstanding evangelical scholar of his generation. Today Dr. Fosdick still has little love for fundamentalism, nor does he acknowledge the validity of its criticism of modernism.

If another example is needed of a modernist tendency to freeze the modernist-fundamentalist debate as the permanent center of ecclesiastical life, we may refer to that influential journal of liberal opinion, *The Christian Century,* which has so unmistakably established fundamentalism as a color word while vindicating a role of ecclesiastical dignity and respect for such terms as liberalism and modernism. The *Century's* outlook today is little different:

* Dr. Fosdick became Professor of Practical Theology at Union Theological Seminary in 1915, after a decade as minister of First Baptist Church, Montclair, N.J. In conjunction with his professorship, he became stated preacher in 1919 at First Presbyterian Church, New York City. Attacked by fundamentalists for disbelief of historic Christian doctrines, he resigned in 1925 to minister in Park Avenue Baptist Church, which became the interdenominational Riverside Church, where he remained until retirement in 1946.

nothing good can come out of fundamentalism; the hope of the Church and of the world is liberalism. Fundamentalist missionaries may die as martyrs, but they are dismissed as misguided; fundamentalist evangelism may strike into the barren churches of our centuries like lightning from heaven, but it is naive and socially irrelevant; fundamentalist scholarship may produce worthy textbooks and religious journals, but they are suspect and dangerous because they are not liberal; fundamentalists may even criticize fundamentalists but unless they defect from evangelical Christianity to liberalism they are still unacceptable. Certain influential liberal sources, no less than some fundamentalist leaders, permanently restrict the fortunes of Christianity to the modernist-fundamentalist controversy.

The modernism of the past generation is therefore still regarded as the essence of Christianity. Liberalism thus confronts contemporary Christianity once again with two important and interrelated issues: (1) Is modernism acceptable as expressive of Christianity?, and (2) Is the Christian church ideally inclusive of both modernists and evangelicals?

Dr. Fosdick gives us a recent answer to these questions, but it is not new. He describes himself as an "evangelical liberal." And he so defines the term "tolerance" as virtually to mean the acceptance "of a church inclusive enough to take in both liberals and conservatives without either trying to drive the other out" (*The Living of These Days*, p. 145). Beneath this plea for a "large-spirited inclusive Christianity" still remains the refusal of "definitions of indispensable belief," since liberals consider them an invalid statement of Christian fundamentals.

In view of recent church history, comment is necessary on Dr. Fosdick's contrast of fundamentalist maneuvering and intolerance with the modernist program of tolerance and unity. References to fundamentalist attempts "to drive the liberals out" seem always to ignore the fundamentalist conviction that liberals, because of unbelief, actually had no genuine status within the church. Dr. Fosdick confesses his personal determination "not to surrender to the fundamentalists the control of the great historic denominations" (p. 163, and boldly acknowledges the subtlety of the modernist strategy: "Our place was inside the evangelical churches . . . claiming our liberty, biding our time" (p. 165). Dr. Fosdick depicts the pressures effecting his own resignation as a modernist as the loss of one battle in a war sure to bring him ultimate victory (p. 149). He concedes, albeit distastefully, "a long process of political intrigue"—of "political maneuvering . . . and . . . questionable compromises" by inclusivist denominational leaders who sought his approval by the Presbyterian Church U.S.A. (p. 149); of an "appeasement" policy which portrayed him "in as orthodox outlines as possible"; of pleas "to rephrase my affirmation of faith, using words with more orthodox aroma" acceptable to conservatives (p. 150). Doubting the honesty of such inclusivist tactics, Fosdick relates his meritorious refusal to conceal the extent of his revolt against orthodoxy. He declined to support an ambiguous recommendation of the Judicial Committee, adopted by the General Assembly, which pleased both sides by meaning one thing to conservatives and another to liberals (p. 170). Alongside the liberal plea for unity and mutual tolerance, therefore, are ranged these indications of modernist awareness of an essential incompatability between modernism and fundamentalism.

Interestingly enough, throughout the modernist-fundamentalist controversy the fundamentalists were indirectly supported in their emphasis on incompatibility and intrinsic differences — for quite other ends than their own — by liberals (especially Unitarians) on Dr. Fosdick's left. They appealed to common honesty as the motivation for liberals to leave the evangelical denominations, inasmuch as the terms evangelical and liberal are mutually exclusive. A *Christian Century* editorial on January 3, 1924, sketched the contrast ably enough: "The difference between Fundamentalism and modernism . . . are foundation differences, structural differences, mounting in their radical dissimilarity almost to the difference between two distinct religions . . . Christianity is hardly likely to last much longer half-fundamentalist and half-modernist." Indeed, if fundamentalism were all that Dr. Fosdick represents it to be – "an urgent peril in all the evangelical churches" (p. 159) – no liberal could in good conscience long tolerate it. Today, on the other hand, the contrast between modernism and evangelical Christianity is being sketched anew from a quite different standpoint by theologians of former modernist sympathies, to show the radical perversion of biblical Christianity of which classic liberalism was guilty.

Modern churchmen who permit only secondary criticisms of it, make the adequacy of classic liberal theology a contemporary issue through continued espousal. Dr. Fosdick himself enumerates certain criticisms: liberalism adjusted Christian thought to the standard of secular culture, so that "the center of gravity was not in the gospel but in the prevalent intellectual concepts of our time" (p. 245); it was "too blind to the tragic sinfulness and plight of man" (p. 248); it took too negative a view of the Bible (p. 243). Although the first of these criticisms would be sufficient to discredit modernism as the bearer of the essence of Christianity, Dr. Fosdick nevertheless refuses to bring the liberalism that he represented under vigorous criticism. While conceding that he "took the optimistic color of our generation" (p. 237), he declines to be classified with main-stream liberalism, or rather with those "extreme" liberals whose views are now under fire (p. 231). There were varieties of liberalism, and his variety, says

Dr. Fosdick, did not share these objectionable features which later invited a criticism of liberalism as secular and non-Christian. He identifies himself with that "very considerable number" of liberals who rejected "automatic, inevitable social progress" (p. 237) ; who denied that the "Kingdom of God could fully come in human history on this planet" (p. 239) ; who refused to reduce Christianity to mere ethicism but widened it rather to include Jesus' world view and his faith in God as well as his morals (p. 242) . While extreme liberalism doubtless propounded an excessive divine immanence, Dr. Fosdick defends his as the New Testament view (p. 253) . Moreover, notwithstanding European criticism and rejection for more than two decades of Dr. Fosdick's diminution of divine revelation to prophetic initiative and insight, he evades any acknowledged support of liberalism's exaggerated confidence in human reason (p. 256) . Although writing appreciatively of neo-supernaturalism's stress on a divine initiative in our religious experience (p. 236) , and on the necessity and primacy of God's self-revelation (p. 256) , and although voicing his debt to Niebuhr for the emphasis that even our best good is corroded by ego-centricity and pride, Dr. Fosdick nonetheless repeatedly declares that his own brand of liberalism (p. 251) is without need of neo-orthodox revision, since he did not join the "optimistic extremes" of other modernists.

Evangelicals will not lament some dangers (such as an excessive divorce of faith and reason, an unhealthy pessimism) that Dr. Fosdick senses in neo-supernaturalism. But protest must be made when he protects Fosdickian liberalism from theological criticism, when he insists that even neo-supernaturalism is best sanctified by liberalism, when he concedes that neo-supernaturalism attracts him in its disavowal of any final theology. Herein an unrepentant liberalism of the 1920s is seeking immortality for itself in the 1950s.

Curiously enough, Dr. Fosdick throughout his lifetime has professed the conditioning of every generation's theology by its social matrix. Therefore, each theology sooner or later is destined for discard (p. 232). "Static orthodoxies," he tells us, "are a menace to the Christian cause" (p. 230). "Theologies are psychologically and sociologically conditioned" (p. 231). "Theological trends . . . are partial, contemporary" (p. 232). "If anything on earth is tentative, it is systems of theology" (p. 231). Explanatory and interpretive theories (of God, the atonement, and so forth) are essential, but "their probable insufficiency must be assumed and their displacement by more adequate ways of thinking positively hoped for." "No existent theology can be a final formulation of spiritual truth" (p. 230). "Dogmatism in theology, whether 'liberal' or 'orthodox,' is ridiculous" (p. 231).

In view of Dr. Fosdick's representations of theology as necessarily relative and changing, is it not incredible that he should wish for his own views a durability and an exemption from criticism which he denies to the views of others? Is it not amazing that Dr. Fosdick is unwilling to refer his own prejudices to this principle of inevitable change, which he has so confidently invoked against the orthodoxy of the past? It was on the ground of the supposed inevitability of theological change that Dr. Fosdick had in fact contended that "creedal subscription to the ancient confessions of faith is a practice dangerous to the welfare of the church and to the integrity of the individual conscience," and, moreover, is "hampering to the free leadership of the Spirit" (p. 172).

Dr. Fosdick even seems to arrogate to his views a veiled prophecy of finality: "Neither the extremes to which liberalism often went nor the extremes to which neo-orthodoxy goes today will be the final word" (p. 265). Are we not, in context, to regard the stable view of Dr. Fosdick as that final word? Yet has he not elsewhere firmly disowned the possibility of any final word in theology? Are we not to expect that, as in the mid-20s he urged the Church to go beyond fundamentalism, and as in the mid-30s he pleaded that "The Church Must Go Beyond Modernism," so in the mid-50s he would require that it go beyond Fosdick? Dr. Fosdick himself complains that other liberals, after rejecting biblical positions, too often fell prey to a static orthodoxy of their own (p. 246). Allegedly, there is no genuine protection from theological relativism. Yet hesitancy and half-heartedness characterize his own application of this concept. Now and then Dr. Fosdick ventures to write not merely of "the basic Christian experiences," but of "revelations of truth"; indeed, he insists that he himself maintains "the timeless values and truths of the gospel" (p. 147), and that liberals agree with the historic denominations "in the abiding substantial truths" they support (p. 163). The impression is unavoidable that Dr. Fosdick more consistently observed the limits of his approach when in decades past he spoke of theory rather than of truth in words like these: "In theology I hold the opinions which hundreds of . . . ministers hold" (p. 172). However halting the application to his personal position, Dr. Fosdick has cut himself off in principle from any privilege to propose lasting truth. And this fact puts us on guard when we overhear Dr. Fosdick, quite indifferent to the limitations of his theory of knowledge, pleading with modernists to stop conforming Christ to contemporary culture, but rather to challenge modern culture in the name of Christ (p. 246). Elsewhere he pleads for "well-thought-out, positive statements of liberal convictions in the realm of Christian faith" (p. 243). But where, within Dr. Fosdick's approach, is the minister to find fixed and final concepts and ideas wherewith to challenge the prevalent intellectual concepts of the times? If the liberal minister is to avoid both a revealed theology and an adjustment to contemporary culture, in the name of what is he to discriminate permanent truths from impermanent opinions? For not only are dogmatic certainty and static creed elsewhere affirmed to be unnecessary and impossible, but dogmatism is dogmatically alleged to be a source of religious ruin (p. 233).

Dr. Fosdick's autobiography reflects the speculative assumptions that determine his readiness to delete the sacred doctrines of evangelical Christianity from his conception of vital religion. Two such controlling prejudices, contradictive of biblical Christianity, stand in the forefront: (1) the notion that man's experience of God is immediate, without a necessary dependence upon past mediation; and (2) the notion of the human mind's incompetence to grasp spiritual realities. It is not amiss to comment briefly on these biases.

Dr. Fosdick writes of "direct, immediate, personal experience as the solid ground for assurance" (p. 234). Stated this bare way, we seem to have here the reiteration of an important Reformation and New Testament emphasis, namely, that Christianity involves no mere second-hand relationship to God. Assurance of salvation is not suspended upon the word of some priest or hierarchy, but rather is subjectively ascertainable through the immediate witness of the Spirit. Actually, however, Dr. Fosdick virtually excludes any historically mediated revelation and redemption in his emphasis on man's present relationship to God. The center of religious experience is shifted to subjective immediacy. Faith in immortality, for example, is simply postulated from the worth and value of man; the human venture is futile unless man's life is fulfilled beyond history. The implications stand out even more fully when we inquire into Dr. Fosdick's conception of the Gospel. He tells us: "The essence of Christianity is incarnate in the personality of the Master, and it means basic faith in God, in the divinity revealed in Christ, in personality's sacredness and possibilities, and in the fundamental principles of life's conduct which Jesus of Nazareth exhibited" (p. 269). Read these words as often as one will, one cannot escape the conviction that Dr. Fosdick's statement contradicts the New Testament view that the essence of Christianity is the good news of the saving death and resurrection of Jesus Christ for doomed sinners (cf. I Cor. 15:1-4). Instead of depicting Jesus Christ as the redeemer of all men, Dr. Fosdick tells us simply that Jesus of Nazareth was the first and finest Christian. The center of Christian experience is so much contemporized in Dr. Fosdick's exposition that it is difficult, in fact, to see why the continuity of our immediate experiences of God with the facts of the Gospels and the life of Jesus Christ need be maintained, or even can be. In the final analysis, Dr. Fosdick not only abandons the mediated redemptive religion of the Bible, but clings to the speculative scheme he shaped to replace it. It is worth noting that in this attachment Dr. Fosdick will find little support and sympathy from contemporary theology. Many able liberal scholars have long since acknowledged the speculative character of this modernist defection, and have repudiated it as a perverse misconception of the essence of Christianity. The tide of theological thought in our day has turned against this view, and acknowledges once again the uniqueness of the Hebrew-Christian revelation of redemption and the centrality of the cross of Christ.

Dr. Fosdick's restriction of the relevance of reason in the spiritual world accounts for his concessions to metaphysical agnosticism. This weakness even the newer neo-supernaturalistic views carry over from the older modernist tradition. It is curious to note Dr. Fosdick's apprehension over Barth's divorcing of revelation and reason, while yet he approves Barth's emphasis that "our concepts are not adequate to grasp this treasure." Nonetheless, Dr. Fosdick disallows us any final theological knowledge; the influence of William James, he confesses, long ago put him on guard against absolutism (p. 323). Yet it is hardly clear that, had Moses and Isaiah and Paul heard the Harvard apostle of pragmatism, they would on his account have surrendered their persuasion of the fixed revelation of the character of God. Dr. Fosdick curiously tells us: "Ideas of God change and ought to, but that fact does not mean that anything has happened to God [how Dr. Fosdick came by this latter bit of fixed information he does not inform us]." Nowhere does Dr. Fosdick harmonize his own incidental references to enduring spiritual truths with his denial of the competency of reason in the spiritual world, and with the consequent assertion of theological relativity. While he appeals deferentially to "the life and words of the historic Jesus" (p. 247), he does not indicate why even those teachings of Christ which pass Dr. Fosdick's censorship are exceptions to the rule that divine truths cannot be infallibly grasped and communicated in the dimension of humanity.

Dr. Fosdick's affirmation of the theological relevance of last-generation liberalism comes as a keen disappointment to many evangelical leaders. Prone to assume that liberalism had been chastened, curbed, and forced to abandon its defenses by the drift of the times, if not by the authority of biblical revelation, these evangelicals will find in Dr. Fosdick's *The Living of These Days* a revelation that he has not really lived through our era with theological awareness; he moves still within the gates of a romanticized experiential Christianity isolated from the realities of history. Casting the fortunes of liberalism in this unrepentant mold will not only evoke wide disappointment, but it will provoke the conviction that the time for theological controversy is once again upon us. Evangelicals will be tempted to speak of Dr. Fosdick in much the same mood as Dr. Fosdick has chosen to speak of William Jennings Bryan: "What he said was nonsense, but the way he said it—his voice, his inflection, his sincerity—was fascinating" (p. 148).

Evangelicals are not alone in their negative verdict on classic liberalism, Dr. Fosdick's species included. Influential liberal circles see the necessity of superseding the Fosdickian views of the 20s if Protestant theology in the 50s is to maintain its vitality. In fact, the whole initiative in theology is now shaped by leaders who dismiss Fosdick's *The Modern Use of the Bible* as a mirror of outdated prejudices. They do not share his reliance on the relevance of classic liberalism, but have already conceded the irrelevance even of the Fosdickian version.

A sound theological instinct supports their uneasiness over the classic liberal position. Even at best liberalism reflected the invasion of a secular spirit. It exaggerated God's immanence, minimized man's sinfulness, concealed Christ's supernaturalness and the centrality of his redemptive work; attached utopian expectations to history, ignored the task of evangelism. For half a generation, most centers of the old liberal thought have been compromising, adjusting, and refurbishing the views of a generation ago. Their theologians and ministers are eager to get beyond the modernist-fundamentalist controversy. For them classic liberal theology was too strongly leavened with secularism to be cherished as a fixed point of theological debate.

The fact that modernism evolved a counter-dogmatics to historic Christianity, a counter-ethics, a counter-ecumenicity, attested the radically different premises with which modernism began. These inevitably spelled out their counter-implications to historic Christianity. That modernism took this course was no reflection on Christianity; it was a commentary, rather, on the fact that modernism quite understood its starting point, rooted in speculation instead of in revelation. What is a reflection on Christianity, however, is that many Protestant leaders did not sense this alien starting point. They chose, rather, to defend it as expressive of the essence of Christianity. Moreover, some influential leaders today still glory in a speculative secular standpoint whose implications are disastrous for the Christian faith. Yet neo-supernaturalists like Barth and Brunner have expressed themselves no less pointedly than did J. Gresham Machen, in *Christianity and Liberalism,* in delineating the intrinsic differences. Barth does not hesitate to speak of modernism as a heresy. "Within the organized unities of the Evangelical Churches we are faced with the fact of pietistic-rationalistic Modernism" in which, he writes, "we do not recognize faith and the church," and in encountering which Christianity is called "to purification, to a rendering of our account, to responsibility." Over against modernism, "although it has neither been expelled from the evangelical churches nor voluntarily gone over to found a counter-church, we draw the line as definitely as over against Catholicism" *(The Doctrine of the Word of God,* Vol. I, Part 1, New York: [Scribner's, 1936] 36ff.).

Note many years after Fosdick delivered his great sermon against the fundamentalists, Brunner was delivering a series of lectures in the United States in which he said bluntly: "A first glance at fundamentalism shows its strength to consist in a negative: its criticism of modernism from the standpoint of Christian faith . . . A fundamentalist, possessed of a reasonably correct knowledge of Christianity, will have little difficulty in proving that the modernist teaches, under the label of Christianity, a religion which has nothing in common with Christianity except a few words, and that those words cover concepts which are irreconcilable with the content of Christian faith" (*The Theology of Crisis*, p. 9. [New York: Scribner's, 1929]).

This first lecture has sketched several facts foundational to ensuing discussions: (1) Present ecclesiastical goals and spiritual opportunities enhance the values of a united co-operative witness. (2) Modernism as the permanently valid norm of Christianity is still a vocal conviction. (3) Evangelical theology on the grounds of Scripture, logic, history, and experience must repudiate it as a perversion of essential Christianity, a conclusion shared even by thinking former liberals. Shall we then regard fundamentalism as the permanently valid criterion of Christianity? or more properly, of a pure biblical theology? Our next lecture probes this pertinent problem in fixing evangelical responsibility in contemporary theology.

CHAPTER TWO

THE FUNDAMENTALIST REDUCTION

LIBERALISM HAS BEEN called a perversion of Christianity. Fundamentalism, on the other hand, has sometimes been stigmatized as a Christian "heresy." Is essential Christianity to be identified with either of these options? May not evangelical Christianity, dissatisfied with both fundamentalism and modernism, transcend the alternatives of the modern-fundamentalist controversy?

Fundamentalism counteracted the modernistic philosophy of religion from the standpoint of supernaturalistic Christianity. Certain essentials that had come under special attack dictated its test for orthodoxy: the authority of Scripture, the deity of Christ, his virgin birth, substitutionary atonement, bodily resurrection and literal return. The temporary test of assent to these specific tenets served its purpose well, for fundamentalism thereby exposed unbelief by boring beneath evasive declarations about the Bible and the supernaturalness of Jesus.

Nonetheless, fundamentalism suffered from its own inherent perils. Concentration on "the fundamentals" often displaced doctrinal responsibilities of the Church in the wider dimensions of historic creeds and confessions of faith. Evangelical pulpits resounded almost exclusively with "the fundamentals" supplemented periodically with "the case against evolution." The importance of other theological indispensables became tragically marginal. The norm by which liberal theology was gauged for soundness unhappily became the skeletal summary of distinctive fundamental doctrine. The inevitable result was a premium on creedal brevity. This, in turn, brought further dangers. The organic relationship of revelational truths was neglected. Complacency with fragmented doctrines meant increasing failure to comprehend the relationship of underlying theological principles. Individual doctrines were reduced to simple clichés, without much thought of their profounder systematic implications.

The fundamentalist movement became a distinctly twentieth-century expression of Christianity, characterized increasingly by its marks of reaction against liberalism. Its theological emphasis and temperament were primarily concerned to correct the social matrix and social philosophy shaped by liberalism. While adhering to "the heart of the biblical gospel" (cf. I Corinthians 15:1-4) in evangelism and missions and Christian education, in its campaign against the so-called "social gospel" fundamentalism at the same time tended to narrow "the whole counsel of God," and felt little obligation to exhibit Christianity as a comprehensive world and life view. In becoming other-worldly in spirit, fundamentalism not only neglected the exposition of Christian philosophy and constructive personal and social ethics, but even became distrustful of such interests. Because it failed to relate the Christian revelation to the broad concerns of civilization and culture, and narrowed the interests of religion to personal piety only, fundamentalism—to borrow words from Dr. G. Brillenburg Wurth in a recent issue of *Christianity Today*—ran the danger "of degenerating into a morbid and sickly enthusiasm" ("Theological Climate in America," Vol I, No. 10 [Feb. 18, 1957], p. 13). Beneath this pietistic tendency lay an uncritical antithesis between the heart and the head to which most fundamentalist educators and ministers subscribed their schools and their churches. This belittling of the intellect, and the phrasing of religious experience primarily in terms of the emotional and volitional aspects of life, is a tendency actually more in accord with the anti-metaphysical temper of modernistic theology than with biblical theology. Nevertheless, many fundamentalists uncritically followed this distinction, despite their insistence on a core of objective spiritual knowledge. In his work on the history of philosophy, *Thales to Dewey* (New York: Houghton-Mifflin, 1957), Gordon H. Clark criticizes Protestant liberalism as a caricature of historic Christianity, but indicates that fundamentalism's narrow disparagement of intellect often leaned in the same direction.

This tendency is prominent among those segments of the movement that lack a genuine appreciation of scholarship. Such circles seldom treat deeper theological issues with scholarly precision, yet they arrogate to themselves at times an unbecoming authority in fields beyond their mastery.

Fundamentalism revealed other disturbing features. It lacked theological and historical perspective. Calvinism and Arminianism it embraced side by side, not alone in polemics against the secular climate of the day, but in an intentional moratorium on discussing doctrinal differences. The result was little mutual devotion to the dedicated enterprise of theological study and research. Impatience and disinterest deterred precise formulations of doctrinal details.

Fundamentalism neglected the production of great exegetical and theological literature. It placed heavy reliance on reprints of the theological classics of the past, from which it derived a borrowed academic strength. This failure to produce scholarly books was due in part to the staggering task of carrying forward on traditional lines the Christian program of missions and evangelism bequeathed by the modernist defection. Another reason for literary paucity was modernism's capture of strategic educational leadership and facilities, while fundamentalism, in its distrust of higher education, did little to encourage and support scholarly graduate pursuits.

Furthermore, fundamentalism veered at times to anti-denominationalism rather than to interdenominationalism. Not content with the promotion of rival non-denominational, interdenominational and super-denominational fellowship and cooperation, it gravitated frequently into caustic criticism of denominational effort. The rift between fundamentalists and modernists became especially pronounced just after World War I, and reached its bitterest point in that decade. The devout effort to preserve the Christian churches from paganizing influences through a searching and scholarly analysis of the alternatives drifted into a reactionary current. The World Christian Fundamentals Association, formed in 1918, although carrying on a positive spiritual program of missions, evangelism, Bible conferences, Bible institutes, and Christian colleges, nevertheless engaged more and more in vitriolic polemics.

Neglect of the doctrine of the Church, except in defining separation as a special area of concern, proved to be another vulnerable feature of the fundamentalist forces. This failure to elaborate the biblical doctrine of the Church comprehensively and convincingly not only contributes to the fragmenting spirit of the movement but actually hands the initiative to the ecumenical enterprise in defining the nature and relations of the churches. Whereas the ecumenical movement has busied itself with the question of the visible and invisible Church, the fundamentalist movement has often been pre-occupied with distinguishing churches as vocal or silent against modernism.

Many fundamentalists, moreover, identified Christianity rigidly with premillennial dispensationalism. Some even were prone to label non-dispensationalists as incipient modernists. Doubtless the premillennial spirit was already in evidence in the very beginnings of the fundamentalist movement eighty years ago, when the Niagara Bible Conference in 1895 first proposed the "fivefold test" to determine ministerial attitudes toward the fundamentals. But it was not until after World War I that fundamentalism became largely a premillennial enterprise. While the editors of the Scofield Bible did not condition evangelical fellowship upon a premillennial confession, a dominantly premillennial orientation was given the evangelical movement through the dispensational emphasis of the Scofield Bible and of leaders of the World Christian Fundamentals Association. Fellowships erected on a broader base, like the National Association of Evangelicals, are required constantly to balance this emphasis.

These fundamentalist features—neglect of the organic interrelations of theology, of the bearing of the Christian revelation upon culture and social life, and of the broader outlines of the doctrine of the Church—exacted a costly historical toll. When the classic liberal theology was at last overtaken by an inevitable judgment and collapsed, fundamentalism, with its uncompromised regard for the authority of Scripture, saw the theological initiative pass not back to the evangelical forces but rather to neo-orthodoxy, a movement fearless to criticize liberalism in terms of both internal philosophical and external biblical points of view. However unsatisfactorily its principles of the theology of the Word and of the witness of Scripture were applied, neo-orthodoxy nonetheless earnestly and aggressively produced a vigorous commentary and dogmatic literature.

In surveying fundamentalism's eighty-year life cycle, one must regret today's contrast to an earlier stature of positive, profound influence. At one time fundamentalism displayed a breadth and concept of theological and philosophical perspective and a devotion to scholarly theological enterprise not characteristic of the present movement. The twelve-volume set, *The Fundamentals,* distributed to the ministry in 1909 as the gift of two evangelical lay leaders, and reaching ultimately a circulation of three million copies, illustrates the fact. A cursory examination of the booklets discloses many evidences of evangelical strength. Here one finds polemic without bitterness, and a concentration upon great issues besides evangelism and missions, important as these are, by the evangelical enterprise. Anyone reading *The Fundamentals* will find an abundant relating of the abiding elements of biblical theology to pressing modern interests.

James Orr of Glasgow discusses the virgin birth of Christ in the opening article of Volume One. He enriched the evangelical outlook on both sides of the Atlantic both through significant books and as general editor of *The International Standard Bible Encyclopedia.* Benjamin B. Warfield, one of America's ablest exegetical scholars, wrote the second article, on Christ's deity. His meticulous theological works still serve the evangelical cause. The third essay, on "The Purposes of the Incarnation," is by G. Campbell Morgan, one of the finest Bible expositors of the past generation. It is noteworthy that both postmillennialist and premillennialist supplied opening articles, united in an evangelical witness to the person and work of Christ. Today's fundamentalist movement, in its present reactionary position and mood, could hardly rally the participation of such representative and distinguished scholars and leaders as the contributors to *The Fundamentals.* With A. C. Dixon and R. A. Torrey as editors, the participants (besides those already named) included W. H. Griffith Thomas, Melvin Grove Kyle, William G. Moorehead, Handley C. G. Moule,

E. Y. Mullins, George L. Robinson, and George Frederick Wright.

No sense of pressure or panic shifts their whole emphasis to the inspiration of the Bible, important as this theme was for contributors like Orr and Warfield, who even prepared separate books on this subject. An article on higher criticism, near the end of the first volume, carefully avoids blanket condemnation of higher criticism as such, and in fact vindicates a positive role for higher as well as for lower criticism. This first volume, indeed, does not end without a resounding emphasis on "the authority and authenticity of the Holy Scriptures," a conviction infusing the entire series. All the contributors believed that the sacred Hebrew-Christian writings must be referred to a special divine activity of revelation and inspiration; all emphasized that in matters of doctrine Scripture is the only reliable and authoritative canon. Yet they were not required to agree "jot and tittle" in their expositions of inspiration, as anyone familiar with the writings only of Orr and Warfield will recognize at once. The fundamentalist movement's later uniformity and rigidity in formulating inspiration resulted from reliance upon clichés more than upon a readiness to define its fuller doctrinal implications. This development contributed needlessly to liberalism's prevailing misunderstanding of the evangelical view of Scripture. Only uncritical and unrepresentative expositions, however, supplied the slightest basis for ascribing to fundamentalists such straw views as belief in a specially inspired King James Version, or in the veritable divine dictation of Scripture. Truly representative fundamentalist expositions, while upholding the normative and trustworthy character of Scripture, refuse to sketch divine inspiration in terms of sheer dictation. The contributors to *The Fundamentals,* in their mutual dedication to supernatural Christianity, retained creative liberty to expound the witness of Scripture to its own inspiration.

Moreover, this attached no legal constraint to conform every detail of these formulations to the conclusions of each other. No premium, of course, rested on disagreement and difference. But Scripture ever remained the conspicuous final authority by which fundamentalist expositions were to be governed and judged. While many American fundamentalists preferred Warfield's statement of inspiration to that of James Orr, yet none doubted the positive evangelical principle of Orr's theological approach. The older apologists appealed confidently to the lordship of Christ and to the witness of the Spirit, being less inclined than recent evangelical thought to rest everything on the bare inerrancy of Scripture. This did not imply their displacement of objective revelation by subjective considerations, for fundamentalism has always resisted modernism's substitution of immediate for mediated revelation. But whether the self-authenticating character of an inspired and authoritative Scripture is derivable from objective indications alone, or whether this self-authenticating character involves also the witness of Christ by the Spirit, was the issue in debate. The older apologetic was less hesitant to begin with Christ —not because it sought to detach Christology from bibliology, but because it sensed the danger that biblicism might seem to ascribe superiority to some principle other than the Christological.

Something of the earlier fundamentalist range and perspective comes from a hasty glance at other volumes in *The Fundamentals* series. The second book, in support of biblical as against critical views, sweeps into the field of archaeology, and closes with a doctrinal essay on justification by faith. An article on inspiration, which begins the third volume, is followed by the testimony of a seminary professor who has rejected his earlier concessions to negative criticism. Between these chapters are essays on the moral glory of Christ, on Christ's revelation of the fatherhood of God, and on the significance of Christian experience. Other volumes present science and Christian faith, the weaknesses of Darwinism, the knowledge of God, the Holy Spirit, sin and judgment, the science of conversion, the nature of regeneration, salvation by grace, the nature of the Church, the efficacy of prayer, the sanctity of the Lord's Day, the Christian use of money, Christianity and socialism, competitive cults and religious movements like Christian Science, Mormonism, Millennial Dawnism, Spiritualism, and Roman Catholicism. The essays indubitably differ in quality, but when one recalls that *The Fundamentals* sought a rather general reading audience, the series creditably reflects a scholarly competence, a refreshing range of interest, an application of biblical Christianity to the wider problems of life and culture, and an avoidance of restrictions and negations frequently associated with fundamentalism in our times. A delightful absence of caustic apologetics and polemics pervades these writings. Restraint is shown toward men of dissimilar views; no attempt is made to depreciate their abilities and skills. A scholarly concentration of evangelical effort on the evidential and apologetic side of Christian supernaturalism characterizes *The Fundamentals.*

In the matter of Christianity and science, the early fundamentalists quite carefully avoided a dogmatic dismissal of the whole scientific enterprise as perverse speculation. Contributors to *The Fundamentals* doubtless agreed on the inadequacy of any explanation of the universe and man in merely evolutionary terms; in this respect they anticipated the dangers of the naturalistic-communistic view of life better than those apostles of "Divine immanence" who merely baptized evolutionary theory with a capital E. Genesis the early fundamentalists regarded as an inspired account of beginnings; they deplored its dismissal as legendary and mythical. At the same time they did not rule out the contribution of science to an understanding of origins. Doubtless most contributors would have hesitated to join James Orr in conceding symbolic and allegorical elements in the Genesis account. Long before his contribution to *The Fundamentals,* Orr had approved theistic evolution in a form that required a divine transcendent activity to shape the distinctive levels of being and life. Some contributors more than others deferred to scientific opinion in supplementing the creation narrative. The message in *The Fundamentals* centers in the great affirmations of the creation narratives. Its support of Christian supernaturalism is wary of whatever threatens biblical theism, and it is certainly not pro-evolutionary. At the same time the writers are neither suspicious nor distrustful of science. They are open to the facts but unconvinced that all the facts have been introduced. Could science actually clarify nature's beginnings, it would ultimately stand face to face with the facts of revelation.

The first edition of the *International Standard Bible Encyclopedia* (1915) carried a lengthy article supporting, and no essay opposing, evolution. The critical reaction of American fundamentalists undoubtedly influenced the editors to include an article countering evolution in the 1929 edition. It should be recalled that naturalism seized the initiative in the American espousal of evolution. John Dewey's claim that evolutionary science had destroyed the foundations of theism and had vindicated the naturalistic interpretation of life was widely accepted. In this context, the case for supernaturalism and against naturalism necessitated a case against evolution. Fundamentalists, however, questioned the factuality of development rather than exposing the inadequacy of evolution. This disposition, to exclude scientific explanations, rather than to evaluate their adequacy, has maneuvered fundamentalism repeatedly into a tardy and retarded awareness of the constantly changing scientific scene. Some fundamentalist popularizers boldly disparaged scientific studies as a whole, using sarcasm and ridicule to reinforce their deficiency of logic. More cautious spirits, however, refused to dogmatize against every possibility of development in nature, and inclined to agnosticism rather than to skepticism in relationship to evolutionary theory. J. Gresham Machen, for example, driven by the biblical view to support miraculous supernaturalism, was disinclined to pose as an authority in geology and biology. Britain launched somewhat of a case against evolution on a scholarly plane, but American fundamentalists expended their energies more in vocal hostility to evolution than in the production of scholarly, meaningful literature. Some evangelicals in America requested of science only that it refrain from tampering with the reality of the supernatural, with the role of transcendent divine power in creating the graded levels of life and the essential uniqueness of man. They did not feel called upon to exclude a scientific supplementation of the Genesis account of beginnings. The main thrust of the fundamentalist interest in science, however, had become mainly anti-evolutionary. Nature as a divine laboratory in which men may read the plan and thought of God, and science as a sphere of divine vocation where Christian young people may facilitate the control of nature to man's purposes under God, were all but lost as motivating concepts.

Outside conservative theological circles, especially among unchurched people and among members of many liberal churches, the word "fundamentalism" became a term of reproach. Secular newspapers and magazines use it today, quite in the Fosdickian spirit, as a badge of obscurantism. This is less than fair to the traditions of the movement as a whole. It is true, of course, that the great bulk of Christian believers in our century, as in any other, are ordinary men and women, not scholars. Even the first disciples have been impugned at times as "illiterate fishermen," and Paul did not hesitate to concede to the Corinthian believers that there were "not many wise" (according to the traditions of speculative philosophy) in the churches. To dismiss the fundamentalist as an obscurantist is a strategy often appropriated by those hostile to belief in the supernatural. It gains credibility in liberal circles through the reactionary spirit of some present fundamentalist segments which seem to align themselves against higher education, science, and cultural interests.

Such reactionary tendencies in fundamentalism, therefore, caused men of profound biblical loyalties to hesitate to identify themselves with the movement as such. They prefer to be called conservatives or evangelicals. They are aware of undesirable connotations of the term fundamentalism. Already by 1923, when Machen wrote his penetrating critique of modernism, *Christianity and Liberalism,* men of his theological acumen preferred to call themselves evangelicals.

The real bankruptcy of fundamentalism has resulted not so much from a reactionary spirit – lamentable as this was – as from a harsh temperament, a spirit of lovelessness and strife contributed by much of its leadership in the recent past. One of the ironies of contemporary church history is that the more fundamentalists stressed separation from apostasy as a theme in their churches, the more a spirit of lovelessness seemed to prevail. The theological conflict with liberalism deteriorated into an attack upon organizations and personalities. This condemnation, in turn, grew to include conservative churchmen and churches not ready to align with stipulated separatist movements. It widened still further to abuse of evangelicals unhappy with the spirit of independency prevalent in such groups as the American Council of Churches and the International

Council of Christian Churches. Then came internal debate and division among separatist fundamentalists within the American Council. More recently, the evangelistic ministry of Billy Graham and of other evangelical leaders, and efforts whose disapproval of liberalism and advocacy of conservative Christianity are beyond dispute, have become the target of bitter volubility.

It is this character of fundamentalism as a temperament, and not primarily fundamentalism as a theology, which has brought the movement into contemporary discredit. Doubtless it is unfair to impute this mood of rancor and negation to the entire fundamentalist movement. Historically, fundamentalism was a theological position; only gradually did the movement come to signify a mood and disposition as well. Its early leadership reflected balance and ballast, and less of bombast and battle. Only later did a divisive disposition show itself, plunging the evangelical movement into internal conflict.

Even at the height of the modernist-fundamentalist controversy, when the late Dr. Clarence Edward Macartney led the Presbyterian Church U.S.A. in the exclusion of Dr. Fosdick because of the latter's defection from the historic doctrines, a spirit of gentlemanliness prevailed. There were spokesmen on the fundamentalist side – and on the liberal side also – who forgot the imperative of love for neighbor in their witness for doctrinal truth. But even Dr. Fosdick, asserting that there were "all sorts of fundamentalists," is compelled to admit that "most fundamentalists were not nearly so pugnaciously reactionary as the liberal portrait of them commonly made them out to be," and he refers to "staunch conservatives who did not agree with my opinions but who were gracious, fair-minded and courteous" (p. 155). Presbyterian opposition to his liberal views, he concludes, was dignified, and reflected "the honest concern of dogmatic minds to keep the church static in doctrine" (p. 154). He pays tribute to Macartney's fairness and courtesy as the leader of evangelical forces in the Presbyterian Church U.S.A. The "vocabulary of invective" used by Dr. Fosdick's Unitarian critics, who stood left of his position, reflects a bitterness and distortion that drives him to admit that Unitarian assaults were as fierce as any by the fundamentalists, even involving "completely untrue" reports about him. Yet Dr. Fosdick manages to recall those attacks "with genial good will" (p. 167).

The recrudescence of fundamentalism during World War II has involved a diversification within the movement's ranks. On one side are those eager to detach the great theological affirmations from a recent negative reactionary spirit and to strengthen constructive theological and ecclesiastical activity; on the other, those who add to reactionary spirit by multiplying divisions and by disowning brethren in the former category. The first group insists that fundamentalists of the latter definition are severing themselves from the spirit of historic evangelical Christianity; the second group maintains that evangelicals of the former category are making a subtle retreat to a compromised fundamentalism.

By mid-century, fundamentalism obviously signified a temperament as fully as a theology. Despite its belligerency, many evangelicals courageously stayed with fundamentalism, remembering rather its contribution to Christianity's age-old battle against unbelief. Others, however, weary of the spirit of strife, wrote off a pugnacious leadership with the declaration that "fundamentalism is dead." None, it should be noted, showed the same courage and earnestness in calling fundamentalism to judgment and repentance as did Barth and Brunner in approaching classic liberalism. Should evangelical leaders as candidly admit the excesses of fundamentalism as neo-orthodox leaders have admitted the excesses of the prevailing liberalism? They dare not do less. The growing revulsion toward the fundamentalist temperament is but one evidence that orthodoxy is being chastened in our day. A renewal of biblical Christianity will involve not only a restoration of the fundamentals, but also a revival of fundamentalists imbued with a new mind-set and a new method in ecclesiastical life.

This second lecture has noted the flaws of fundamentalism. Although upholding a theology corrective of the modernist misrepresentation of Christianity, fundamentalism evidenced faults of its own: (1) Interest in the isolated fundamentals often concealed the organic sweep of biblical theology and minimized the comprehensive exhibition of Christianity as a world-life view. (2) The Gospel was often narrowed to personal and pietistic religious experience, in which the spiritual role of the intellect is disparaged, and the social and cultural imperative of Christianity evaded. (3) Neglect of theological research, especially in systematic theology, led to fragmentation over secondary positions, especially in eschatology, which were elevated to primary importance. (4) Protest against modernist leadership in major denominations gravitated easily toward reactionary anti-denominationalism and to a spirit of ecclesiastical independency neglectful of the biblical doctrine of the Church except in relation to the issue of doctrinal purity. (5) In these tendencies recent fundamentalism dissipated the vigor of its own classic heritage which half a century ago, was marked by largeness of perspective and spirit, prized creative scholarship above entrenched clichés, and conditioned theological fellowship upon the firm acknowledgment of the final authority of Scripture more than upon an achieved uniformity in all doctrinal minutiae. (6) Recent fundamentalism generally has approached science on the edge of an anti-evolutionary temper, whereas a more positive and comprehensive outlook shaped the theological exposition of the created world in earlier decades. (7) Reactionary traits so dominated fundamentalism in this generation that it acquired a reputation not simply for its theology of conservative biblicism, but for its temperament of negation, strife, and lovelessness.

If modernism stands discredited as a perversion of the scriptural theology, certainly fundamentalism in this contemporary expression stands discredited as a perversion of the biblical spirit.

CHAPTER THREE

THE CONTEMPORARY RESTORATION

IN SEEKING the evangelical imperative in contemporary theology, we have been impelled to disown both the modernist perversion of biblical theology, and the fundamentalist reduction of it as well. Nevertheless, we would regret thereby to suggest that as theological expressions little choice exists between these movements. Modernism is a phase of the historical tide of unbelief. Fundamentalism, despite its problems of temperament, is a theology reflective of biblical supernaturalism in the conflict against the unbelief of modernism. Therefore we particularly need to understand fundamentalism in its theological formulations. In so doing, we may clarify our personal responsibility – to divorce biblical supernaturalism from its stigma of temperament – and to know it for what it reflects in truth: the unchanging realities of special divine revelation.

Most recent literature dismisses fundamentalism in terms of temperament and ignorance. Little significance is given to the movement as biblical supernaturalism in continuing conflict with theological unbelief. Expositions of fundamentalism by non-fundamentalist writers fail to fix attention upon the enduring elements of Christianity that it defended. A few exceptions, who sensed that the role of Christian doctrine was the basic issue at stake, seem almost monumental on this account. Theodore G. Soares, for example, in *Three Typical Beliefs* (Chicago: The University of Chicago Press, 1937), states the issue unabashed: "Fundamentalism is as old as the Reformation, though the name is of recent origin. The differences that have separated the Protestant sects have been peripheral; the great doctrines of orthodoxy have been central, held by all. About half a century ago the inroads of liberalism caused the conservative elements in all the denominations to draw together. They made common cause against what they felt to be a common foe. Asserting that there could be no compromise on the unchanging fundamentals of the Christian faith, they adopted as a rallying cry the name of 'fundamentalist.' They claimed that they were reaffirming the faith as Luther held it, and Calvin, and Knox, and Robinson, and Bunyan, and Wesley, and the great missionaries and evangelists, and most of the theologians until very recent times. And in that claim they were undoubtedly correct. The great Protestant creeds enunciated the doctrines which are now called 'fundamentalist' " (pp. 37f.).

Likewise Edwin A. Burtt, in his *Types of Religious Philosophy* (New York: Harper & Bros., 1939, rev. 1951), is noteworthy for grasping the issue as a fixed doctrinal requirement that fundamentalism supported and modernism scorned. Whatever its weakness, fundamentalism's theological affirmations embraced a segment of doctrine continuous with apostolic and Reformation Christianity. Even a cursory examination of Calvin's *Institutes of the Christian Religion,* to select but one of Soares' references, shows that the great Reformer devotes no less than one in four pages of his first two books to the so-called "fundamentalist" themes – four chapters (I, VI-IX) to the knowledge of God in Scripture, and ten (II, VI-VII, X-XVII) to the God-manhood of Christ, including the virgin birth, atoning death, bodily resurrection, and ascension and visible return. It is hardly accurate, therefore, to depict the modernist-fundamentalist controversy as rising from an attempt to freeze church doctrine "in terms which the fundamentalists chose" (Fosdick, *The Living of These Days, p.* 157). The fundamentals are integral to historic Christian doctrine, and to the sacred Scriptures to which dogmatic theology appeals.

This fact of doctrinal soundness in the struggle with modernism compelled men who were not fundamentalist in temperament or in affiliation to defend the movement, despite many justifiable criticisms, and even to associate themselves with its championing of biblical defenses. Ned B. Stonehouse points out, in his biographical memoir on J. Gresham Machen, that while "not precisely described as a fundamentalist at all," Machen avoided a reputation as a critic of the negations and novelties of the fundamentalist movement, and even contributed a newspaper article on the assigned topic "What Fundamentalism Stands For Now" (*The New York Times,* June 21, 1925) . Since fundamentalist obduracy was being widely invoked as a smokescreen to obscure modernist heresy, it took courage for leaders to speak in its behalf. But many publicly ranged themselves on its side, in preference to an ambiguous detachment that obscured their attitudes toward the historic Christian beliefs that liberalism scouted. For over against modernism's abandonment of the miracles of Christmas and Good Friday and Easter, and of a sacred view of history and of the Bible, fundamentalism stood firmly on the side of scriptural theology and the historic Christian faith.

One of the remarkable turns in the theology of the recent past is that theologians who once shared the liberal viewpoint, and dogmatically excluded from the essence of the Christian religion doctrines like the deity of Christ, his virgin birth, substitutionary atonement, and bodily resurrection, now confess that this perspective was gained from a standpoint of secular unbelief. The marked swing to a greater theological conservatism today involves increasing emphasis on a central and indispensable core of Christian doctrine.

So much is being made of necessary doctrinal preaching and doctrinal faith that the ultimate possibility of a transverse split may again threaten Protestantism through diverse views of the significance of theology. Unrepentant modernist forces strain to journey beyond the modernist-fundamentalist controversy in order to eliminate conflict over creeds. Unswerving evangelicals, on the other hand, consider the liberal revolt against creeds and confessions already discredited, and therefore regard the modernist-fundamentalist debate as an anachronism. The ambiguities of this situation inevitably seek clarification in contemporary discussions of ecumenical unity.

Revival of a doctrinal Christianity eventually must sharpen the ecclesiastical question, as it always has throughout Christian history. Those who disparage Christian doctrine must face a very practical question: Does honesty permit one to continue in a church constitutionally committed to the exclusive support and propagation of specific theological tenets?

Not in medieval times alone, but in early church history as well, Christian faith stood guard against heresy. Christianity even disowned heretical churches and groups of churches (e.g., the Marcionite, Donatist, and Arian congregations). Faced by the Reformation, Roman Catholicism stamped the Lutheran and Calvinistic churches as heretical. Their rejection of the authoritative papacy, their appeal instead to the sole authority of Scripture, became Protestantism's indictment of Rome. In the twentieth century the heresy of Protestant modernistic leavening has become an almost universal problem. The readiness to impose tests of doctrinal acceptability is not an ugly innovation of the fundamentalist movement. Such tests were already a part of traditional confessions of faith. In all ages the Church has faced the question of belief and unbelief, of doctrinal fidelity and infidelity. By her alignments she marks herself either as merely professing or as truly regenerate.

Today's increasing stress on doctrines essential to biblical Christianity coincides in many respects with the doctrinal emphasis of the fundamentalist controversy. No fact of recent Protestant theology is more conspicuous than its emphasis that apart from the clear recognition of the supernaturalness, nay the deity, of Christ, only the shadows of Christianity remain. It is gratifying, moreover, to hear Karl Barth affirming that the church has no liberty to consider the doctrines of the virgin birth and empty tomb optional.

Since 1927 Barth has championed the virgin birth of Jesus Christ against almost a century of speculative doubt and denial by the liberal tradition, and likewise against such contemporaries as Brunner within his own neo-orthodox tradition. Of the virgin birth Barth writes: "The Church knew well what it was doing when it posted this doctrine on guard, as it were, at the door of the mystery of Christmas. It can never be in favour of anyone thinking he can hurry past this guard . . . It will proclaim as a church ordinance that to affirm the doctrine of the Virgin birth is a part of real Christian faith" (*The Doctrine of the Word of God,* Vol. I, Part 2, p. 181). Barth's comments on Brunner's position on the virgin birth are even somewhat reminiscent of the older criticisms directed by fundamentalists against modernist denials of a generation ago: "Brunner's denial of the Virgin birth is a bad business. As is also the case with Althaus, it throws an ambiguous light over the whole of his Christology." Indeed, he even echoes sympathetically the complaint of Berdyaev: "When I reached the passage in which Brunner confesses that he does not believe in Jesus Christ's birth of the Virgin, or at least confronts it with indifference . . . it seemed to me as though everything had now been cancelled, as though everything else was now pointless" (*ibid.,* p. 184).

Barth even writes: "It is no accident that . . . the Virgin birth is paralleled by . . . the miracle of the empty tomb. These two miracles belong together . . . The Virgin birth at the opening and the empty tomb at the close of Jesus' life bear witness that this life is a fact marked off from the rest of human life . . . Marked off in regard to its origin: it is free from the arbitrariness which underlies all our existences. And marked off in regard to its goal: it is victorious over the death to which we are all liable" (p. 182). "We shall have to meet attack on the *natus ex virgine* with the further reflection that by it an indispensable connection is destroyed which is actually found in the creed, so that the *tertia die resurrexit a mortuis,* too, is actually called in question" (p.183). Moreover, "if we confess that Christ is risen and risen bodily, we must also confess it to our own future resurrection" (p. 117).

While Barth assuredly does not affirm all that an evangelical doctrine of atonement requires, he quite properly widens the concept of substitution to apply to the active as well as the passive obedience of Jesus Christ, and he speaks of the sinless Christ who suffers in our stead (p. 152), bearing the wrath of God which must fall on sinful man (p. 157). Barth writes that God "takes upon Himself the sin and guilt and death of man, that laden with it all He stands surety for man" (p. 378). He writes of "the humanity of Jesus Christ . . . characterized by the bearing of our sins" and "abandoned to punishment, suffering and death" (p. 428). While he disallows organizing the whole of dogmatics around the atonement, rather than around Christology in the wider sense, Barth thinks it incontestable that the atonement belongs to those central considerations of dogmatics of which "we must not lose sight even for a single moment" (p. 873). Indeed, he acknowledges that "with the doctrine of the atonement, we come to the real centre . . . of dogmatics and Church proclamation" (p. 882).

The doctrine of Christ's second coming likewise belongs to essential Christianity. In his earlier writings Barth's eschatological teaching was leavened by an excessive contrast of historical time and eschatological time. This contrast has been modified somewhat, if not yet satisfactorily, by way of reaction to Bultmann's consignment of the Christological events to myth and symbol. Barth now stresses that the Church exists on earth in the interval between the ascension and the second coming (p. 692f).

Even with respect to Scripture as the norm of Christian doctrine, Barth has given us many statements which, as far as they go, have an evangelical ring and rigor. The Church, he tells us, is created and maintained by the Word of God, and is governed by that Word: "by the Word of God in the form of the testimony to the revelation of God in Jesus Christ set down in Scripture. To say that Jesus Christ rules the Church is to say that Holy Scripture rules the Church" (p. 693). Whether Barth really succeeds in his intention is debatable enough, but we must not miss the dramatic force of the fact that "in contrast to Roman Catholicism and Protestant modernism" he aims professedly to derive the answer to the question of revelation from the Bible (p. 457). Barth not only asserts the priority of the Scriptures over sources of divine knowledge affected by the Fall, but he says bluntly that "if the Church dared simply to abandon the sign of the Bible dominating its worship and instruction, it would be the end of Protestantism" (p. 460). Indeed, he even acknowledges that "the right doctrine of Holy Scripture" "must always be sought and found in exegesis and therefore in Holy Scripture itself" (p. 462).

The dramatic element in this theological reversal is simply this: in the first third of our century theological initiative lay with those who labeled the defenders of these doctrines as obscurantists; today, in contrast, the prominent theological thrust defines the discard and neglect of these doctrines as violence to Christianity. A basic fundamentalist thesis has been vindicated: the intrinsic genius of Christianity demands proclamation of doctrines that fundamentalism upheld in the controversy with liberalism. Barth's basic theme is triumphant grace in Christ. He casts human crises in the context of divine redemption. He rejects a merely modalistic view of the Godhead. Emphasis on the atonement finds its center once again in the substitution of the Servant of the Lord for sinners. From the standpoint of a vagabond liberalism, such concepts reflect an evangelically oriented framework toward which contemporary theology is being propelled.

It would be overstatement to imply that in the recovery of these doctrinal emphases Barth and the neo-orthodox theologians return in all essentials to an historic evangelical exposition. That is not the case. Doubtless Barth in a crucial hour strategically exposed the inner weaknesses of classic liberalism to its own constituency. Doubtless he raised long-neglected evangelical doctrines to a position of earnest theological importance and study. On the other hand, his present theological position revolts against elements in both Reformation and biblical theology.

Perhaps G. C. Berkouwer has given the most constructive critical evangelical appraisal of Barthian theology in

The Triumph of Grace in the Theology of Karl Barth (Grand Rapids, Eerdmans, 1956). Without in the least depreciating Barth's refutation of the older modernism, Berkouwer addresses most pertinent questions to Barth's "theology of the Word of God," lest we uncritically assume that the Barthian plea for a Christological-Christocentric theology presents a thoroughly evangelical and biblical exposition of revealed sovereign divine grace in Christ. Berkouwer reminds us that the Marcionite, antinomian, perfectionist, universalist, and Roman Catholic expositions of this same plea are speculative and quite objectionable. Philosophical categories in the Barthian exposition of creation, election, reconciliation, and eschatology leave Berkouwer quite convinced that the triumphant grace motif in this neo-orthodox form compromises biblical theology and blunts the purity of the gospel. Only with caution, therefore, may the evangelical speak of a debt to Barth.

Important motivational differences distinguish the neo-orthodox from the fundamentalist interest in doctrine. Neo-orthodoxy has no intention of reinstating a fixed and final theology. Indeed, it refuses even to concede that biblical theology is revealed. Doctrines, even prophetic and apostolic doctrines, are treated as devout theological reflection, not as revealed theology. The reinstatement of "biblical theology" on this non-revelational level gains various shadings today. In the radical theology of Bultmann "the fundamentals" are revived as an integral part of Christian faith understood as myth rather than as historical fact. While Barth acknowledges more and more the historical interrelations of faith, his repossession of biblical theology involves no renewal of the traditional confidence in divinely revealed doctrines.

Beneath this halting return to the Bible lurks a dialectical prejudice that imparts an anti-intellectual turn to the neo-orthodox view of divine self-disclosure and hence to its definitions of revelation and inspiration. God's revealing activity is sketched in terms of personal encounter beyond the grasp of human concepts, therefore sealing off any divine transmission of truths and words. Nowhere is the Barth-Brunner theology more disappointing than in thus exalting Schleiermacher's objectionable definition of revelation. Indubitably neo-orthodoxy has supplemented and modified Schleiermacher's view in numerous details. Its essential point, however, is retained, that God discloses no truths or doctrines concerning himself and his purposes. Nowhere does neo-orthodoxy's loud claim to honor the witness of Scripture fall upon stonier ground than in its attempt to justify this anti-intellectual prejudice from the Bible. The evangelical exposition of inspiration has been nearer the heartbeat of the Bible when, in debating the relative merits and defects of the dictation, verbal, and concept theories, it at least has held the line against anti-intellectual speculations about divine revelation and inspiration.

Contrary to conservative reliance on an authoritative Bible, the neo-orthodox doctrinal interest retains the liberal methodology. Barth still maintains the requirement, already stated in his early writings, that the Bible as such be distinguished from divine revelation (p. 463). Deference to biblical criticism compromises the religious finality of Scripture in the historic evangelical sense. To more than one interpreter Barthian dogmatics seems indeed marked for frustration in endeavoring to preserve the Bible as the witness *of* revelation, while at the same time restricting it as a witness *to* revelation. For this controlling postulate cannot survive the test of Scripture's implications and assertions about itself. Here again, evangelical theology, insisting that the Divine Logos and Speech comes in human conceptions and words—how else could it be revelation?—is assuredly on the side of the biblical witness.

Barth indeed speaks of the "inspiringness" of the Bible, of its character as a frame wherein one is confronted by the encountering Christ. He fails, however, to acknowledge the inspiration or "inspiredness" which the New Testament ascribes to Scripture (II Tim. 3:16), and on which evangelical theology therefore insists. The many passages in which the Old Testament prophets claim to convey the very words of God gain from Brunner the grudging admission of "a low order of revelation." Yet nowhere does he reconcile this concession to verbal revelation with his basic theory of revelation as uncommunicable in concepts and words. Barth, to be sure, tells us in a refreshing passage that "the biblical texts must be investigated for their own sake to the extent that the revelation which they attest does not stand or occur, and is not to be sought, behind or above them but in them . . . If it is asked whether Christianity is really a book-religion, the answer is that strangely enough Christianity has always been and only been a living religion when it is not ashamed to be actually and seriously a book-religion" (pp. 494 ff.). Often his writings disclose a concern for textual and exegetical considerations that renegade liberalism had snubbed, and that even yet is lacking in some neo-orthodox theologians. Yet when Barth expounds what Scripture teaches about its own inspiration, he reflects the prejudices of dialectical theology. The dialectical evasion of the rational and verbal coherence of the Bible circumvents a doctrine of the inspiration of Scripture that corresponds to the witness of Scripture itself.

Presumably to serve God's sovereignty—an objective that evangelical theology accomplished in quite other ways—Barth breaks with the high view of the Bible. He evades inspiration as the work of the Spirit in "the emergence of the spoken or written prophetic and apostolic word as such" (p. 517). Professedly to preserve divine freedom, he disallows the transmutation of God's Word into human speech. Barth rightly stresses that the present illumination of the Spirit is necessary. For the swift appeal to the Bible does not of itself resolve all theological uncertainties. The Bible itself can be invoked in a quite independent and autonomous way; its sacred text may be bent to subserve speculative, subjective, and emotive preferences, at the expense of sound exegesis. But Barth wrongly invokes the witness of the Spirit to offset the need for stabilizing the words of Scripture as the Word of God. Nowhere does Barth really prove his case that the traditional view interposes the Bible as a "paper Pope" between Christ and the Church. Actually the modernist compromise of the authority of the Bible enabled critics to usurp the Lordship of Christ in the theological realm.

There is a further consequence of deserting the high view of inspiration. Scripture itself loses the right to delineate the essential elements of the person and work of Jesus Christ. Although neo-orthodoxy calls for a revival of biblical theology, its formulation of Christian doctrine stresses whatever allegedly agrees with the revelation of the person of Christ. And evangelical theology must show enthusiasm for the Christocentric phrasing of revealed theology. But in neo-orthodoxy this principle operates critically and selectively in evaluating the data of Scripture. Scripture thereby no longer serves to refract what coheres with Christ's person. Consequently, subjective factors constantly threaten the construction of Christian doctrine. This is seen in Brunner's indifference to the doctrine of the virgin birth, despite Barth's assertion that "the narratives of the Virgin birth were admitted to share in the gospel witness because of a certain inward, essential rightness and importance in their connection with the person of Jesus Christ"

(p. 176). It is seen also in Brunner's indifference to the empty tomb in relation to faith in Christ's resurrection, whereas Barth is not content to declare the Easter story "quite indispensable to the whole, impossible to think away, the subject whose predicate is all other narratives." He notes, rather, that "its most illuminating moment" according to Mark's Gospel "consists in the inconceivable fact of an empty sepulchre" (pp. 114f.), and that this outward sign guards against reducing resurrection from an event to a speculative idea (p. 179).

Barth's speculative premises about divine self-revelation not only shape his departure from the historic view of Scripture, but determine also his general attenuation of evangelical doctrines, including his bias against the exposition of propitiation in the doctrine of atonement. Whenever convenient, neo-orthodoxy does not hesitate to shift its appeal from the nature of Christ to the witness of Scripture. But because the evangelical principle of the organic unity of the Bible is compromised, the dialectical approach accomplishes only a limited return to biblical theology and provides only a relative opposition to liberal theology. A crucial illustration is the hesitancy of dialectical theologians to maintain the full identity of Jesus of Nazareth with the Christ; the historical Jesus is for them a "witness" to the Christ. Here the detachment of the Christological from the scriptural principle actually threatens the central faith of the New Testament, namely, that Jesus of Nazareth is the zenith of divine self-revelation.

Nonetheless, the new theology properly rejects the liberal doctrine of extreme immanence, to which the central Christian concepts had been conformed or had been deleted. The neo-orthodox statement of divine transcendence, however, appears reactionary. Whereas this new formulation of transcendence readmits some traditional and biblical fundamentals (*e.g.*, the virgin birth, the bodily resurrection), it excludes others (*e.g.*, propitiatory atonement) through its stress on God in his self-revelation as being "always Subject, never Object." An exaggerated doctrine of divine transcendence is as harmful to the fortunes of biblical theology as an excessive doctrine of divine immanence. While the one reinstates elements which the other disallowed, it also repudiates elements which the other accepted. Twentieth-century theology incorporates this vulnerable approach to Scripture with speculative preconceptions of either divine transcendence or immanence. By imposing this procedure on biblical data, some elements of scriptural theology are accepted, others rejected. Actually the limits of transcendence and immanence are fixed by all, not merely by some, Bible events and doctrines. It is this totality which guards against speculative distortions. Only the preservation of the total scriptural revelation justifies a theology's claim to be biblical. Genuinely biblical theology views the divinely inspired Scriptures as the font from which, and from which alone, a trustworthy and adequate statement can be derived of those important and essential elements whose inward connection with the person of Christ must be maintained.

Unfortunately, fundamentalism paid scant attention to basic principles with which its theological positions were integrally connected. Had evangelical theology pursued the tasks of Christian philosophy, emphasis would not have been placed upon isolated doctrines. Skillful evaluation of modernism required more than the exhibition of its doctrinal denials. It involved as well the exposure of the rationalistic bias or philosophical prejudice that underlay this unbelief, especially the secular formula of exaggerated divine immanence involving an unbiblical doctrine of revelation and reason in religious experience. This underlying speculative bias not only tempered isolated doctrines but pervaded the entire structure and outlook of Christian theology. Denial of the "fundamentals" involved at the same time a modification of the biblical view of God, man, nature, history, and redemption. The Hebrew-Christian world-life view was equally at stake in other doctrines not listed by the fundamentalists. In the modernist denial, was not the doctrine also of particular providence in jeopardy? In the absence of a sensitivity to Christian philosophy, the recent reinstatement of isolated fundamentals conceals their simultaneous distortion by an unbalanced doctrine of transcendence.

Neo-orthodox theology has enlivened present theological discussion with a new, and rather wholesome, sensitivity to divine confrontation. The Christianity of the twentieth century had quite obscured the God who continually encounters and confronts man. Modernism had exchanged the divine initiative in special revelation for the human quest for God. Fundamentalism had stressed Christian experience dominantly in terms of doctrinal assent and outward social restraints, appended of course to an initial experience of rebirth whose vitality was to be renewed in periodic crises of spiritual surrender. Ritualistic churches dulled the edge of divine-human encounter through their recital of good news in a form which often struck modern men as monotonous and impotent. Twentieth-century man was face to face with death at every moment; if Christianity was to retain its relevance for him, it must somehow preserve him each moment face to face with life, with the ultimate, with God. The contemporary approximation of the New Testament emphasis on spiritual immediacy as preserved by the religion of the Mediator is therefore a gain. We who minister to this tensed generation dare not neglect the continual unveiling of God in Christ encountering every lost soul in creation, preservation, conscience, judgment, and the call to repentance and faith. Nor dare we neglect the sway of the confronting Christ over our own souls, framed by creation and refashioned by redemption primarily for a life of personal fellowship in his service. The disregard of this dimension of Christianity has doubtless done more to provoke the rise of modern religious cults than any other factor.

At the same time, the incessant neo-orthodox laboring of the theme of confrontation and encounter secretly betrays a weakness. This neo-orthodox travail follows from the failure to adequately correlate the dynamics of present Christian experience with New Testament revelation. The fundamentalist confidence in a specially inspired communication of the knowledge of God and his purposes is sound. The Bible shielded fundamentalism from theological relativism despite the inroads which secular thought achieved in modernistic Protestantism. The theological plight of modernist theology is a commentary on history's inevitably adverse judgment on religious convictions not built on transcendent foundations. Scripture is not reducible to exalted religious insight; it is a literature of theological conviction uniquely shaped within an orbit of special divine revelation and inspiration. Nay, it is more; it is the normative and authoritative statement by which Christian faith and doctrine must be tested.

Evangelical theology might have discharged the tasks of Christian philosophy compatibly with its retention of an intellectualistic view of revelation. The superiority of the evangelical view does not exempt the movement from a relevant exhibition of its positions, but obliges it the more. Indeed, a fresh exploration of the interrelations of revelation and reason (in view of man's possession of the image of God created and sullied, and renewed in redemption) is one of its present imperatives. In the next lecture we shall consider others. At best we may stress that the greatness of evangelical theology dare not be merely discussed in an academic vacuum, nor in the comparative privacy of the churches. It must be demonstrated in the arena of personal and social struggle, and amid the heat and fire of modern culture in turmoil.

In this connection the historic Augustinian-Calvinistic conception of the relation of revelation and reason holds magnificent relevance for a generation reaching for a transcendent God, while yet concerned for the rational integration of all life's experiences. Modernism's surrender to the secularization of science, of education, and of cultural pursuits generally resulted directly from separating these spheres from the claims of revelation. The way in which theology defines the relationship of revelation and reason will color its comprehension of Christianity and culture, Christianity and science, Christianity and philosophy, no less than the exposition of Christian doctrine and apologetics. If divine revelation stands in essential contrast to human reason, or if it impinges only dialectically upon the human mind, so that divine revelation cannot be grasped in concepts and words, then a Christian philosophy is a vain hope. It is part of the glory of evangelical theology that it rises above the modern contrast between God-truth and world-truth which divides human reason and precludes the intellectual integration of all experience.

The recovery of interest in special divine revelation is one of the gracious providences of our century. It comes significantly at a time when the world must contend with the tactical initiatives of Communism and of irreligion. Protestant modernism succeeded in deflecting Western Christianity's theological interest from biblical revelation to natural theology. This retrograde idealistic philosophy only briefly resisted a further decline to humanism. Evangelicals once reveled in the divine oracles; the modernists now asked whether God exists. Modernism's surrender of biblical revelation finally enmeshed American Christianity in the loss of the self-revealed God; in the non-communist world, as well as the communist, naturalism surged to ascendancy.

Now that special revelation is once again recognized as integral to Hebrew-Christian redemptive religion, it becomes a duty of evangelical theology to conserve this gain, and to shield it from misunderstanding. A sense of spiritual urgency must motivate evangelical theology both in its world program of evangelism and missions and in its cultural impact.

It is to the credit of evangelical Christianity that it has never defined its primary responsibility to be the unfruitful task of reorganizing unregenerate society. Rather, it has throbbed first to the heartbeat of the Great Commission in its program of individual rescue and enlistment. Then it has uniquely and strategically registered the social impact of Christianity. The message of divine creation and redemption thus comprehends both the individual life in its private growth and the redeemed man in all his social and cultural life. The awareness of biblical revelation as relevant to the whole of life grants contemporary civilization the living prospect of a rationally satisfying explanation of human aspirations and problems.

This third lecture places the real strength of the fundamentalist movement in the relationship of the fundamentals to the theology of revelation. Evangelicals outside the orbit of fundamentalism were attracted by its biblical supernaturalism. While dissenting from fundamentalism's unattractive aspects, evangelicals did not withhold theological endorsement of its struggle against doctrinal unbelief. The central fundamentalist doctrines ranged the movement against the modernist assault upon scriptural positions in defense of historic and biblical Christianity. Liberal interpreters minimized this bond of fundamentalism with the

Bible and the historic creeds of Christendom. Instead, they fixed attention on the objectionable temperament, on structural deficiencies, on academic and spiritual deficiencies of the movement. But recent theology, in contrast with the liberal disparagement of the "five points," has once again restored fundamentalist emphases as central elements of serious doctrinal study in relation to essential Christianity. While contemporary formulations frequently halt short of a fully biblical treatment, they nevertheless involve the recovery of long-neglected doctrinal considerations. Neo-orthodox reaction against the excessive liberal doctrine of divine immanence reinstates erstwhile disputed positions. It threatens other biblical elements, however, because the contrary view of divine transcendence conforms more to speculative than scriptural requirements.

Any current theology worthy to be called Christian vindicates the propriety and indispensability of the deity, virgin birth, substitutionary death, bodily resurrection, and second coming of Christ. Even the new appeal to the witness of Scripture, although set in the context of a defective view of revelation and inspiration, has a hopeful side. It remains for evangelical theology, however, to reinforce the still inadequate positions to which Barth and Brunner have lifted much of the prevailing theological outlook by setting forth the basis and content of sturdier biblical claims. Evangelical theology's best hope for a relevant and aggressive impact in our turbulent times lies in a bold, biblical emphasis on the relationship of revelation and reason.

CHAPTER FOUR

THE EVANGELICAL RESPONSIBILITY

A HIGHER SPIRIT to quicken and to fulfill the theological fortunes of this century will require more than the displacement of modernism, more than the revision of neo-orthodoxy, more than the revival of fundamentalism. Recovery of apostolic perspective and dedication of the evangelical movement to biblical realities are foundational to this hope. The vigorous application of redemptive Christianity to modern life is a complex and staggering task. For this, evangelical forces need to cultivate multiple areas of enlargement.

I.

Evangelical theology has nothing to fear, and much to gain, from aligning itself earnestly with the current plea for a return to biblical theology. To measure this moving front of creative theology sympathetically, to understand its concern and courage, and to name its weaknesses without depreciating its strength will best preserve relevant theological interaction with the contemporary debate. "Evangelical Christianity has reason neither to resist the call for a theology of the Word of God, nor to speak with contempt of the new emphasis on the witness of Scripture. It has no license to stifle voices that call for hearing the scriptural testimony anew." Reactionism can only reflect on evangelical Christianity's own stake in the biblical witness. The one legitimate question the evangelical movement may ask is: Does the theology of crisis actually pass this biblical test? It has no complaint against Brunner's verdict that "the fate of the Bible is the fate of Christianity," although it may be called to adduce evidence that Brunner impairs both Scripture and the Christian religion. The evangelical movement must show that Christian theology is more earnestly and profoundly biblical than dialectical theology. But let it not fail to make its very own the passionate concern for the reality of special divine revelation, for a theology of the Word of God, for attentive hearing of the witness of the Bible, for a return to biblical theology.

II.

Rededication to positive and triumphant preaching is the evangelical pulpit's great need. The note of Christ's lordship over this dark century, of the victory of Christianity, has been obscured. Great preaching is more than moving oratory and personal counseling. If it be evangelical, preaching must enforce the living communication of the changeless realities of divine redemption. The basic doctrines too often have been set in a context of negative preaching. To assert the truth of revelation in the face of denials means little without applying its awesome lessons to life. Positive achievements and values of the Christian faith have been too little evident, crowded out at times by a spirit of theological and apologetic vengeance, or of unbecoming polemics. The minister whose pulpit does not become the life-giving center of his community fails in his major mission. Perspective on Christianity's current gains and final triumph will avoid a myopic and melancholy discipleship.

Without lessening the transcendent judgment of the message of revelation and redemption upon the present course of this world, the Christian pulpit must present the invisible and exalted Head of the body of Christ; linked to him, this earthly colony of heaven moves to inevitable vindication and glory. Already in this world the triumphant powers of the future age are being reflected in this spiritual fellowship. The perplexing problems of our perverse social orders find their hopeful solution only in this regenerative union. Out of its spiritual power must spring the incentive to creative cultural contributions. The beggarly fundamentalist modification of worldly patterns and the consequent tendency of Christianity to be merely a parallel effort disclose the need for new life and vigor. Christian enthusiasm is the only permanent tonic for pessimism. The Easter faith retains power to charm a wayward and weary world. When preacher and pulpit are burnished in bright hope, luster will be restored to the people in the pews. The biblical message is one of hope beyond judgment. Driven into hiding by the constant threat of doom, a man's spirit can be liberated by the prospect and promise of worthwhileness. Today this affirmative and triumphant note must be sounded. The risen Christ and his radiant Church must become the fulcrum of local society, of this entire age, and of the world.

III.

The evangelical fellowship needs a fresh and pervading conception of the Christian life. Too long fundamentalists have swiftly referred the question, "What distinguishes Christian living?" to personal abstinence from dubious social externals. The Christian conscience, of course, will always need to justify outward behavior in home, in vocation, in leisure. But Christian ethics probes deeper than external negations. It bares the invisible zone of personality, where lurk pride, covetousness, and hatred.

Unfortunately, fundamentalism minimized the exemplary Jesus in the sphere of personal ethics, for three reasons: (1) concentration by conservative theology on the redemptive death of Christ, in view of modernism's inadequate doctrine of atonement; (2) reaction against the liberal contraction of Christian ethics to Jesus' moral life and teaching; and (3) the fundamentalist reduction of personal ethics to simple negations.

Blemishes in liberal Christology cannot, of course, be minimized. Virtually the whole modernist tradition denied or misstated the deity of Christ and often ambiguously distinguished his humanity from our present sinful nature. Nor would we charge fundamentalism with disinterest in the earthly life of Christ. It defended the details of that life against critical assaults on the Gospels. It championed Christ's sinlessness and moral purity. It prized his virtues of piety and prayer, love, meekness, patience under reproach. In his dealings with men, Jesus of Nazareth demonstrated the perfect combination and balance of qualities elsewhere only approximated. But much of the relevance of that perfect humanity to our manifold relations with God and with fellow men was obscured in fundamentalism's stress on the deity of Christ. The fundamentalist interest in the ethics of Jesus too hesitantly connected his moral experience with the everyday experience of Christian believers. The theme of Christ's oneness with God was developed so exclusively in terms of his deity that the import of his dependence upon God for all human nature was lost. The manhood of Jesus is essentially one with ours, but its uniqueness is in the zone of sinlessness, not of humanness. His uncompromised devotion and dependence upon God, his sustained relationship of mutual love, embodied the ideal pattern of human life in perfect fellowship with God.

In view of his unbroken union with God, his humanity holds a central significance for all humanity.

In this light, a new importance attaches to the Nazarene's learning of the Father's will in the course of obedient dependence. His struggle with dread temptation to magnificent victory over all the assaults of evil, his exemplary trust, his unwavering reliance on God even in the darkest hours, his interior calm of soul, the wellspring of love that flowed from his being – in all these experiences Christ models for us an ideal spiritual relationship with God, a religious life whose very thought and desire and will are the Father's. In Jesus of Nazareth, God is fully resident; in God, Jesus is fully at home. He lives out the "rest in God" that actualizes the "abiding" to which we are called. He exhibited in human flesh those uncompromised divine qualities, especially righteousness and love, which mirror Godhead. As he is history's only instance of perfect humanity, he publishes God's intention for man both in creation and in redemption. He embodies the goal of human nature wholly indwelt by God, of manhood so fully resident in God that they share one moral life.

Another way in which evangelicals need to move beyond the fundamentalist ethic is in comprehending the whole of the moral law in fuller exposition of love for God and neighbor, and in the larger experience of the Holy Spirit in New Testament terms of ethical virtue. Often quite legalistically, and with an absoluteness beyond New Testament authority, fundamentalism's doctrine of surrender, of rededication, has merely proscripted worldly practices from which the believer was discouraged. Unemphasized, however, are the fruits of the Spirit and those many virtues which differentiate dedicated living in terms of biblical Christianity. While in Christ alone God is seen in the flesh, and while even redeemed men dare not expect an absolute immanence of God in finite experience, nor aspire to divine sonship in the full and unmediated sense of the eternal Son of God, nonetheless the moral inspiration and force of the life of Jesus of Nazareth must not be neglected.

IV

We need a new concern for the individual in the entirety of his Christian experience. He is a member of all life's communities, of faith, of the family, of labor, of the state, of culture. Christianity is by no means the social gospel of modernism, with its many shades of utopian expectation from unregenerate human nature. It is nonetheless vibrant with social implications as a religion of redemptive transformation. To express and continue the vitality of the gospel message, marriage and the home, labor and economics, politics and the state, culture and the arts, in fact, every sphere of life, must evidence the lordship of Christ. Even the believer's use of time, whether waking or even sleeping in this barbiturate age, is of concern to Christ, and therefore to God's people.

Obviously, the social application of Christian theology is no easy task. For one thing, fundamentalism fails to elaborate principles and programs of Christian social action because it fails to recognize the relevance of the gospel to the social cultural sphere. Modernism defines Christian social imperatives in secular terms and uses the Church to reorganize unregenerate humanity. Its social sensitivity gave modernism no license to neglect the imperative of personal regeneration. Evangelistic and missionary priorities, on the other hand, gave fundamentalism no license to conceal the imperative of Christian social ethics. Despite the perils, no evasion of responsibility for meaningfully relating the gospel to the pressing problems of modern life is tolerable. Not since apostolic times has the world sagged as in our century into the lap of paganism. If Christianity fails now to affirm the sovereignty of God in the marital, financial, political, and cultural realms, these areas will capitulate to secular and speculative programs.

The divine life is a "being in love," a social or a family fellowship in which personality expresses the outgoing, creative relationships of redemption. These emphases carry peculiar significance for believers in our times. A worker by God's creation, man sees vocation therefore as a divinely entrusted stewardship by which to demonstrate love to God and service to man. As divinely ordained, the state declares God's intention and the dignity of man's responsibility for preserving justice and repressing iniquity in a sinful order. This world challenges man to interpret literature, art, music, and other media in reference to eternal order and values.

V

Evangelical confidence in the ontological significance of reason makes possible a positive, courageous approach to science. For more than a century and a half modern philosophy has regrettably minimized the role of reason. Kant disjoined it from the spiritual world. Darwin naturalized and constricted it within the physical world. Dewey allowed it only a pragmatic or instrumental role. These speculations took a heavy toll in Christian circles. A segment of evangelical Christianity nonetheless maintained its insistence upon the Logos as integral to the Godhead, the universe as a rational-purposive order, and man's finite reason as related to the image of God.

Yet for more than a generation the evangelical attitude in scientific matters has been largely defensive. Evolutionary thought it met only obliquely. American fundamentalism relaxed in traditionalism. It often neglected scrutinizing its own positions in the light of recent historical and scientific research. It even failed to buttress its convictions with rigorous theological supports. For this reason the movement has suffered blanket dismissal as a reactionary refusal to revise the Christian faith in keeping with contemporary scientific convictions.

Yet modernism, despite its eager pursuit of such revision, achieved no true correlation of Christianity and science. While modernism adjusted Christianity swiftly to the prevailing climate of technical conviction, its scientific respect was gained by a costly neglect of Christianity's import to science. Dr. Fosdick, lampooning the Scopes trial, flays the fundamentalist effort to banish the teaching of evolution from the public schools as imperiling the public interest. Yet nowhere does he sense the peril in the liberal assault on biblical supernaturalism and the consequent dismissal of the Bible from the public schools. Indeed, Fosdick's entire volume contains no reference to John Dewey, who during the Fosdick era infused the whole public school system with a naturalistic philosophy from Columbia University Teachers College in the very shadow of Fosdick's pulpit.

No progress can be made in mutual understanding as long as the fundamentalist impugns the modernist theology as a deliberate betrayal of Christianity to pagan speculation, or the modernist caricatures fundamentalism as simply an obscurantist revolt against contemporary learning.

In purpose the modernist was as concerned to preserve the compatability of Christianity with the scientific understanding of the universe as the fundamentalist was to preserve the identity of essential Christianity with biblical theology. Neither fully succeeded; modernism often championed as scientific truth much that was sheer speculation, while fundamentalism often exalted as revealed theology much that was actually an imposition on the biblical records.

Today a new mood pervades the scientific sphere. That mood may not fully validate the evangelical view of nature, but it does at least deflate the pre-suppositions on which the older liberalism built its bias against the miraculous. Science today is less self-assured that nonspiritual factors account wholly for man. It more earnestly probes features that distinguish man from the animal world. This does not yet, however, involve a return to the Hebrew-Christian view of man and the universe. Even the increasing emphasis on man's uniqueness in view of divine creation is usually sketched in relation to evolutionary theory with distressing ambiguity. But the evangelical movement is now given a strategic opportunity to transcend its hesitant attitude toward scientific endeavor, and to stress the realities of a rational, purposive universe that coheres in the Logos as the agent in creation, preservation, redemption, sanctification, and judgment.

The ramifications of revelation and reason are wider, however, than science, for they embrace all the disciplines of learning. The evangelical attitude toward education itself is involved. The day has now vanished when all the levels of learning, from primary to university, were in the service of God. Two out of three of the colleges now existing in America were founded by the churches. Although only a remnant of these today hold forth the Christian view of life, they pay indirect historical tribute to an era when Christianity held the initiative in education, both in its philosophy and in its practice. The evangelical tradition needs to recapture this spirit of academic ardor. For Christianity cannot long thrive in an atmosphere in which mass education is allowed to repress and impugn Christian confidence and conviction. The distinguished liberal churchman John Baillie, in a biographical essay on the life of his brother, the late D. M. Baillie, makes the passing comment: "I have often reflected that parents who dutifully bring up their children in the traditional orthodoxy which has never submitted itself to the challenge of Renaissance and *Aufklärung,* and who send them to a school whose whole ethos is of humanist inspiration, seldom realize the extent of the spiritual stress and strain to which they are thus subjecting them" (*The Theology of the Sacraments,* p. 14 [New York: Scribner's, 1957]). Dr. John Baillie is not concerned to perpetuate the traditional orthodoxy in which he was indoctrinated in boyhood, but those concerned to do this, and to preserve the impact of biblical and Reformation theology in our century ought to reflect with equal earnestness upon the point he makes. Christianity must not withdraw from the sphere of education, but must infuse it with new spirit and life. To do so requires meeting the challenge of the Renaissance and Enlightenment head-on. In the clash, Christianity need evade neither truth nor fact, for it offers an adequate view of the universe in which we are driven daily to decision and duty. Exposition of the Christian view becomes relevant from the cradle to the grave. In answer to the present secular perspective in public education, shall evangelicals establish private Christian schools? Or shall they rather work for eternal verities within the present public school order, or perhaps even pursue both courses? One fact is certain: evangelical neglect of education will imply the irrelevance of historic Christianity to the pressing problems of the contemporary academic world.

VI

The evangelical movement needs also the sustained study of the New Testament doctrine of the Church and a greater concern for the unity of regenerate believers. Its program of reflecting the unity of the body of Christ in contemporary history is adequate in several regards.

(1) Evangelical discussions of the unity of the Church are shaped to protest the modern inclusive movements. More than the New Testament conception, as a model to be followed, evangelical ecclesiology is concerned with the ecumenical framework as a compromise to be avoided. Ecumenical Christianity blesses a cooperation broader than the New Testament fellowship; it needs to be reminded that not all union is sacred – that the more inclusive the union, the greater the danger of compromising and secularizing its Christian integrity. By contrast the evangelical movement easily restricts cooperation more narrowly than does the Bible. It must learn that not all separation is expressive of Christian unity. The principle of separation itself may acquire an objectionable form and content, related more to divisive temper than to theological fidelity. In the face of the inclusive church movement, the evangelical spirit reacts too much toward independency. The perils of independency are as disastrous as the perils of ecumenicity. Through refusal to cooperate with believers whose theological conservatism and experimental dedication to Christ are beyond question, evangelical Christianity stands in danger of divisiveness and disruptiveness.

(2) Evangelical insistence that the unity of the body of Christ requires a basic doctrinal agreement and a regenerate membership is sound. The ecumenical temperament encourages the breakdown of denominational barriers at too great a price whenever it minimizes doctrinal positions. Interdenominationalism in our century has sprung from a peculiar assortment of motives. Fundamentalists stimulated denominational desertion through discontent with theologically inclusive programs ventured by liberal leadership in the established denominations. While such interdenomina-

tional effort operated on principles broader than those of any one participating denomination, it endeavored to preserve the purity of the evangelical witness by stressing items jeopardized by some denominational programs. Interdenominationalism of this kind is not in actuality an antithesis to denominationalism, since denominational tenets are not called into question. Indeed, most evangelicals prefer to support New Testament programs within their own denominational lines, allowing interdenominational cooperation to spring from multidenominational dedication to common evangelical priorities. The compromise of priorities in denominational circles, however, led to interdenominationalism at the expense of denominationalism; it quickened the sense of an extradenominational unity, to which the life of the denominations as such was no longer considered integral, based on common doctrine and faith.

In the case of Dr. Fosdick and the liberal forces he represented, the interdenominational urge had a different motivation, namely, a virtual depreciation of denominationalism as an unworthy sectarianism insofar as any fixed creedal positions are affirmed. During the modernist-fundamentalist debate, when pressures were on Dr. Fosdick at New York's First Presbyterian Church to become a Presbyterian rather than a Baptist, he had "no sectarian loyalties" that would have made the change difficult, he tells us. His main reason for hesitancy was the formal Presbyterian requirement of a definite creedal statement. This "new freedom with which Christians could disregard denominational lines and work together" (p. 173), the "adventure into unrestricted interdenominationalism" (p. 183) and into the "non-sectarian, inclusive church" (p. 196), was conceived with disdain and contempt for fixed doctrines, and in the ultimate hope, as Dr. Fosdick relates, of a large-scale national and world union of denominations (p. 197). This exaltation of the experiential unity of the Church through the disparagement of the doctrinal soundness of the Church is the great peril of ecumenical ecclesiology today. It dares to proclaim as members of the body of Christ some who do not wear the New Testament badge of identification. Its constant danger is the elevation of the concern for unity above the concern for truth.

Exposition of the nature of the Church, if it is to allay the deepest reservations in American Christianity, dares not ignore an evaluation of these competitive approaches to denominational and interdenominational cooperation.

(3) Evangelical emphasis on an indispensable doctrinal basis for church unity needs, however, to be defined with greater precision. Such concern accounts for evangelical uneasiness over the creedal vagrancy of the World Council of Churches whose nebulous emphasis is only on "Jesus Christ as God and Saviour." Since the evangelical movement includes churches that are both creedal and noncreedal in heritage, a specific creedal unity has not been elaborated, although common theological tenets are listed. Baptist churches, for example, defer to no creed but the Bible, although historically they have held confessions of faith in high regard. (Dr. Fosdick details his association with Baptists — "a church which has no authoritative written creeds and . . . gives to each congregation autonomous control over its own affairs" [p. 159]—indifferent to the Baptist insistence on the final authority of the New Testament.) This evangelical listing of a doctrinal minimum raises difficulties for creedal churches, inasmuch as they consider no article of faith dispensable. To Reformed churchmen, evangelical formulas often appear inadequate and open to objectionable development. They prefer a strictly Reformed and creedal fellowship, a restriction that excludes progress toward the unity of diverse evangelical elements.

On the other hand, the evangelical failure to fully elaborate essential doctrines has resulted in fragmentation by granting priority to secondary emphases (*e.g.*, in such matters as eschatology). Evangelical Christianity has been slow to establish study conferences in biblical doctrine, to encourage mutual growth and understanding. Ironically, study sessions on theological issues are often associated with movements whose doctrinal depth and concern are questionable. The significance of Christian doctrine, its dispensability or indispensability, its definition as witness or revelation, the elements identified respectively as core and periphery — these are issues on which evangelical Christianity must be vocal.

(4) Evangelical Christianity too frequently limits the term "evangelical" to those identified only with a limited number of existing movements. This needlessly stresses a sense of Christian minority and discourages cooperation and communication with unenlisted evangelicals. But the tensions of American church history in this turbulent century cannot be automatically super-imposed upon all world evangelical communities. Ecumenical leadership in the Federal Council of Churches and its successor, the National Council of Churches, failed to reflect the viewpoint of that considerable genuinely evangelical segment of its constituency. In the World Council of Churches, leaders on the Continent also have often found themselves theologically far to the right of American spokesmen, and have found American evangelicals in the World Council disappointingly unvocal. Long before the establishment of organizations like the World Evangelical Fellowship, many European churches had approached the World Council in quest of an enlarging evangelical fellowship. Evangelical world alternatives to inclusive movements arose after most large historic denominations were already enlisted in the World Council.

Does evangelical loyalty within these committed denominations necessarily depend upon the public repudiation of the World Council, and upon their entrance instead into minority movements quite withdrawn from the stream of influential theological discussion? Does such a condition virtually require churches and denominations to withdraw from the arena of relevant ecclesiological debate? Does a proper sensitivity to historical perspective "write off" Anglican and Lutheran, as well as many Reformed groups, as "a lost cause" simply because they are currently unidentified with movements that seem extraneous to their witness and endeavor? Despite its 40-denomination membership, even the National Association of Evangelicals in the United States must accept the absence of Southern Baptists and Missouri Lutherans, whose antipathy for theological inclusivism keeps these denominations also outside the National Council. Many earnest evangelicals are active in the World Council of Churches; many are active outside the National Association of Evangelicals and similar agencies.

The question that obviously remains, of course, is whether an evangelical who prefers identification with the broader movements can justify his participation, if he knows his own spiritual heritage, except in the capacity of a New Testament witness? Must not a silent evangelical in this climate always ask himself whether the silence which once perhaps was golden, now, through a dulling of love for truth and neighbor, has become as sounding brass or tinkling cymbal? Indeed, must not the evangelical always and everywhere address this question to himself, in whatever association he is placed?

Lack of evangelical communication across the lines of inclusive and exclusive movements is not wholly due to the exclusivists. Although proficient in establishing communication with those friendly to the inclusivist ideal, ecumenical enthusiasts have encouraged neither fellowship nor conversation with exclusivist evangelicals. This coldness contributed needlessly to the fundamentalist suspicion of all outside their own constituency, and did little to mitigate the incivility that some fundamentalists reserved for such individuals. The unity of the believing Church requires communication between evangelicals on a basis of mutual tolerance and respect. One achievement of Billy Graham's evangelistic ministry is the prominence given not to an organizational but to a theological principle, namely, that unregenerate humanity is forever doomed apart from regeneration by the Holy Spirit and faith in the substitutionary and propitiatory death of Christ.

(5) Unfortunately for the evangelical cause, the concern for the unity of the Church is now largely associated in the public mind with the inclusive ecumenical vision. If any New Testament doctrine is unmistakably clear, it is the teaching of the unity of the body of Christ. Moreover, the unity of Christ's body is an evangelical motif. Yet the failure of evangelicals to hear what the Spirit says in the New Testament to the churches has created the void now being filled by inclusivistic conceptions of unity. The evangelical church needs to be the evangelical church indeed, needs to search the Scriptures with new earnestness touching the unity of the body of Christ, needs with new earnestness to seek unity in its fragmenting environment, needs to reflect to the disunited world and to the disunited nations the sacred unity of this body.

Although evangelicals have criticized the broad basis of ecumenical merger and unity, they have achieved in their own ranks few mergers on the theological-spiritual level they espouse. Without conceding that denominationalism is an evil, or that the health of the Church increases in proportion to the reduction of denominations, may there not be evidence that evangelical Christianity is over-denominationalized? If doctrinal agreement enhances the deepest unity of believers, may we not expect progress in the elimination of unnecessary divisions by emphasizing the spiritual unity of the Church

This question is complicated by the fact that even denominations with a predominantly evangelical constituency have been committed by some leaders to inclusivist programs. And, by reaction against inclusivist propaganda pressure for merger, evangelical interest in merger has been repressed. Merger on strictly evangelical lines is stigmatized as disruption by some inclusivist leaders who themselves have compromised both denominational and evangelical distinctives. Evangelical Christianity, if it takes seriously its own emphasis on the unity of the body, must therefore show visible gains in demonstrating that unity in contemporary church life.

(6) Contemporary Christianity would gain if the discussion of ecclesiastical tolerance were set in a New Testament context. The scriptural respect for individual liberty in matters of religious belief must not obscure definite requirements for identification with the body of Christian believers. Beyond all doubt, the New Testament upholds specific doctrinal affirmations as indispensable to genuine Christian confession. In this biblical setting, divisiveness is depicted primarily as a theological question, not (as is usually the case today) as a matter of ecclesiastical attitude and relationship. The modernist tendency to link Christian love, tolerance, and liberty with theological inclusivism is therefore discredited. Modernist pleas for religious tolerance and the caustic indictments of fundamentalist bigotry often were basically a strategic device for evading the question of doctrinal fidelity. This flaunting of tolerance, however, was discredited when inclusivist leaders suppressed or excluded evangelicals not sympathetic to the inclusive policy. The "tolerance plea" swiftly dismissed as divisive what was not clearly so in fact. Divisiveness meant disapproval of the inclusive policy, tolerance meant approval. But the New

Testament does not support the view that devotion to Christian liberty and progress and to the peace and unity of Christ's Church is measured by the devaluation of doctrine in deference to an inclusive fellowship. From the biblical point of view, doctrinal belief is a Christian imperative, not a matter of indifference.

Whenever it professes a genuine regard for the scriptural point of view, the inclusive movement is driven to soul-searching in respect to doctrinal latitude and its own propaganda for organic church union. It is necessary, of course, to distinguish personal preferences from official pronouncements. If the ecumenical movement were bound officially to all the opinions of all its constituents it would be a tower of Babel. Yet the situation is not entirely relieved by such a distinction. For if one lists the distinguished churchmen honored as presidents of the World Council, and assumes that this company is regarded not only as ecclesiastically acceptable but as exemplary, much the same problem confronts us in the matter of ambiguous and objectionable views of the significance of doctrine and of the nature of the Church. Within the World Council, in contrast with the National Council, exists a forum from which this ambiguity can be challenged. Evangelicals in this movement, if they bear an evangelical witness, must constantly call the Commission on Faith and Order to judge the theological and ecclesiastical question from the standpoint of Scripture.

(7) The fact must not be ignored, however, that different evangelical conceptions of the visible Church are prevalent. Although historically the Christian churches have all insisted upon a minimal theological assent for admission to membership, Reformed churches share Calvin's view that even in the Church wheat and tares – believing and professing Christians – will dwell together until their final separation in the judgment. Baptist churches have traditionally placed greater emphasis on a regenerate membership

and on a pure church. From the perspective of Baptist history, the formation of the General Association of Regular Baptists and of the Conservative Baptist Association is significant not simply as a protest against a drift toward theological inclusivism, but because so many years elapsed before the Baptist tradition of regenerate church membership and a pure Church was reasserted. Baptist protests against inclusivism need not have taken the form of these particular movements involving denominational fissure, but their concern nonetheless springs from a devotion to the Baptist conception of the Church. Even the disciplinary procedure of the more broadly conceived Reformed churches considers church members flouting or indifferent to creedal standards as guilty of grave sin. Christian churches in the past stressed both a minimal requirement for membership and a maximal indulgence for avoidance of discipline or exclusion. But modernist leaders asserted the inevitability of doctrinal change. Biblical theology and historic creeds and confessions, they argued, could be approved by modern minds only with "mental reservation." Heresy trials became an oddity in contemporary church history, not because of an absence of heresy, but because of the lack of zeal to prosecute heretics.

To fix responsibility in theology, in the things of God, is no human prerogative. God alone, in his self-revelation, has the right to etch his imperatives upon the conscience and heart of creatures called into being for a unique life of fellowship and service. We may be sure that theological responsibility is ultimately evangelical, that it headlines the evangel in its proclamation. For God is self-revealed as the heartbeat of nature, both in its daily providences and in the miracles of Christmas and Easter; he is self-revealed in Jesus Christ, both in that he was nailed to a cross and could not be held by death; he is self-revealed in Scripture, which cannot be broken. We dare not own any other authority over life and deed but the living God. We dare not own any other God than the righteous and merciful God revealed in Jesus Christ. We dare not own another Christ but Jesus of Nazareth, the Word become flesh who now by the Spirit is the exalted head of the body of believers. We dare not own any other Spirit than the Spirit who has breathed out Scripture through chosen men, so that doubt may vanish about what God is saying to the Church and to the world. We dare not own any other Scripture than this Book. Let other men proclaim another god, another Christ, another spirit, another book or word—that is their privilege and their peril. But if once again the spiritual life of our world is to rise above the rubble of paganism into which it is now decaying, it will be only through the dynamic of revelation, regeneration, and redemption, through the sacred message which once brought hope. We have a task to do, a task of apostolic awesomeness; let us rise to the doing. The hour for rescue is distressingly late.

INDEX

HIEBERT LIBRARY
3 6877 00090 4507